Blackgirl on Mars is a rare bool
introspection, Brown's lyrical
that it almost makes you forget the very deep, guttur- —
violent lessons within its pages.

As both a scholar and a true student of the world, Brown imbues *Blackgirl on Mars* with her intelligence as well as her heart. "The journey of healing is not an isolated affair," Brown poignantly and pointedly states. By weaving her own personal history into Our History as human beings all inhabiting this same precious Earth, she entices the reader to face their own lineage and the part we have all played in the collective trauma that remains. And how we are all, always, searching for home.

ELISA DONOVAN, ACTRESS AND AUTHOR OF
WAKE ME WHEN YOU LEAVE

Lesley-Ann Brown has a brave voice and a keen eye, offering an unflinching view of what it means to be a Caribbean American woman living in Europe.

GARY YOUNGE, AUTHOR OF *ANOTHER DAY IN THE DEATH OF AMERICA: A CHRONICLE OF TEN SHORT LIVES*

BLACKGIRL ON MARS

BLACKGIRL ON MARS

Lesley-Ann Brown

Repeater

Published by Repeater Books

An imprint of Watkins Media Ltd

Unit 11 Shepperton House

89-93 Shepperton Road

London

N1 3DF

United Kingdom

www.repeaterbooks.com

A Repeater Books paperback original 2023

1

Distributed in the United States by Random House, Inc., New York.

ISBN: 9781914420283

Ebook ISBN: 9781914420290

Printed and bound in the United Kingdom by TJ Books Limited

For Christian-Mohammed

Contents

Prologue

Some names of people and places have been changed to accommodate the fantasies of the writer.

When I left Denmark on a cold January evening in early 2019, there was no way of knowing that my grandmother would pass in just two months, leading me back to Trinidad, or even that a global pandemic was hovering out there on the future's horizon. I had read articles suggesting that the melting of our polar ice would mean the release of viruses from bygone eras and noticed specific public figures bringing up the prospect of a pandemic quite often. Still, most of us were not prepared.

When I flew out of Kastrup airport in Copenhagen, there was no return date on my ticket. For this journey of exploration, I am wearing my grandmother's brown hat with the ear flaps. I also have my copy of Masanobu Fukuoka's *The One-Straw Revolution* packed snugly between my clothes and spices. This book will accompany me to every city and country that I visit. I'm in love with the title and the message: Fukuoka is a scientist who experienced a nervous breakdown at his job in the city; he returned to his father's farm in the village to recuperate and reevaluate his life. There, he began an intimate relationship with the plants around him and developed a chemical-free, no-till, intuitive method of cultivation that calls for working with the earth, as opposed to modern agriculture practices such as growing monocrops and using chemical fertilizers. Moreover, he demonstrated that once this relationship is (re)established, it is relatively self-sufficient. As a result, his no-till, chemical-free rice yields surpassed all others in his village.

I carry this book around because, in some way, it describes the life that I want. I am tired of city-living — even a small city such as Copenhagen seems too large for me now. How do I cultivate a simpler life, a life that's more aligned with my health? A life that is more aligned with supporting this planet?

I want to do my part in healing the earth. I live very simply: I enjoy cooking at home rather than dining out, I prefer knitting my own sweaters as opposed to buying them. In my way, I attempt to make as little impact on the environment as possible — I rarely eat meat and try not to buy unnecessary things. I prefer to wear pre-used clothes when possible and up/recycle often. I don't enjoy shopping — a pursuit that only seems to further disorient me. Still, I have to admit that sometimes, when I'm close to sadness and Aldi, I walk the aisles in awe at the sheer abundance of crap available, and often leave with trinkets whose workers I wonder about.

But back to Fukuoka. I was lucky to once work at a farm in southern Denmark — in the Nykøbing Falster area — where Fukuoka's method was implemented. Through WOOF (the World Organization of Organic Farmers), I had the opportunity to find and volunteer on a beautiful farm with free room and board. The farm, which once grew onions, was owned by a man who inherited it from his parents and whose wife, Hannah, taught me how to bake bread. It was late spring, and the small farm was abundant — using no chemicals — in squash, tomatoes, peas, lettuce, spinach and so much more. It was like having your greengrocer in your backyard. Two huge Hungarian pigs ensured nothing went to waste. I played with my guitar (as opposed to simply *playing* it — I don't know how) in my trailer at night, and during the day did things such as clean the chicken coop, prepare various berries and fruit for preservation, hang baskets of garlic up to dry in the barn and put up fences. I wanted to stay there forever.

On more than one occasion, I've also wondered if Fukuoka's "do-nothing farming" philosophy could be applied to life, if one could structure one's life such that each movement facilitated the next effortlessly, using what was around you in the most natural way possible. As I set out on my journey — leaving Denmark to travel throughout the States — I placed this question in my heart for safekeeping.

***

If for some reason you were to end up in my classroom, one of the first things you'd hear me say is that, although I'm your teacher, I expect to learn from you as well. For me, the optimum classroom is an intricate ecosystem where, under the best circumstances, each element can blossom and thrive at what its particular strengths are. I see my role as teacher being that of a "conductor" — in both the physical and the musical senses. It doesn't matter if you're from a Copenhagen suburb or a country on the other side of the globe — we all have things we can teach others, stories to share. In a world that is currently battling a pandemic of social isolation (not to mention a pandemic that *demanded* social isolation), human-to-human contact, allowing us to feel as if we are part of a community, is the best antidote. *Inc.com* reports that social isolation negatively impacts our health. According to some studies, social isolation can be as lethal as smoking thirteen cigarettes a day. Those without healthy social connections have a 50% chance of dying prematurely.

I don't want to suggest my classrooms have been perfect ecosystems of learning, however. My classrooms exist within a system, and whatever happens in that system affects my classroom.

A crude example of how systems within systems affect each other is the so-called refugee crisis, which is a direct result of our Western military and political decisions. This can be seen in the young student who has found herself in my classroom having fled the war in Syria and learned that her education is meaningless here. She attends school to get on track, but as she is about to finish up, changes are made in parliament, which mean there is still more for her to do before she can be accepted into this system. Or it can be seen in a Danish student whose parents had to flee Chile during the US-sponsored military dictatorship of Pinochet. Or in the young Afghan student who you will learn walked to Denmark from his motherland, like so many other young boys whose parents sacrificed them in desperation, hoping that the world would receive them, love them and support them in ways all humans should, but who, due to budget cuts made at the parliamentary level, have now found themselves having to sit in classrooms despite crippling anxiety and lacerations across their small arms.

But it's not about perfection in my classroom. I'm looking to create a space where all of my students, even those with crippling anxiety, can feel, at the very least, comfortable. I strive to do this through *mutual comprehension*, through our innate desire and need to be in community in safe places — through storytelling that is centered around perspectives and experiences and by using the power of *counter-storytelling* to heal.

What many of my past students have had in common, no matter their origin, is a high level of unresolved trauma. It could be the emotional shock of war, the distress of displacement, drug abuse or even feelings of extreme emotional alienation, which themselves could lead to other problems including health issues. It could be any number of countless things that, whether in isolation or cumulatively, can render our nervous systems unable to meet even basic everyday requirements like showing up to class. My number-one priority as a teacher has always been to have a space where students feel valued and safe, as this is integral not only to learning but to living.

***

I know that, by learning more about my students, I learn more about the world, and by extension about my place in it — our place in it — and hopefully you will too. Through my students, I have learned about what growing up in a group home here in Denmark can be like and even why a student from the Middle East would admire Donald Trump. I've learned about many countries, like Eritrea and its history with Yemen, as well as other historical intrigues in countries far away, which some of my students have been forced to flee.

For me, education is not merely about the subject at hand but is also about our *relationship* to learning — do you understand that learning is a process, that it's not just about what you walk into my classroom already knowing but about acknowledging what you don't know? That to truly own knowledge we have to experience it?

Unfortunately, by the time many of my students reach me, they have already been traumatized by their previous educational experiences and have received the message that school is not for them. This is why just having a previously closed-off student smile when they enter my classroom is a victory for me.

I have worked as a teacher for over ten years and have a complicated relationship to this profession. On the one hand, I love being a teacher, although it is definitely one of the most challenging jobs I have ever done. On the other hand, I can't escape the reality that our education system causes a lot of harm to students who are already vulnerable.

I was blessed to have my share of brilliant teachers throughout my education. What all of my favorite teachers had in common was a healthy distrust for the dominating narrative. I was drawn to education because I recognized the true transformational potential it holds. I know this from my own experience in school. Labeled a gifted-learner, my academic excellence had just as much to do with my interest in school as it did with experiencing how my successes positively informed my life. Performing well academically endowed me with a new perspective on what I could do.

I got into teaching because I recognized that, under the right circumstances, the classroom could be a space where you can inspire your students to see the potential in their lives — something that is deeply difficult to access if you are experiencing anxiety and/or depression. It can be a space where we challenge each other to find out who we really are. This can be an exciting and revealing project to engage in with a classroom of young adults.

It is in my classroom that I've learned so much more about the social intricacies here in Denmark that tend to get obscured by the seemingly large, Keynesian-inspired, mostly state-employed middle class, and about those lives that have been deemed "collateral damage" by the US government.

In my classroom, I am often the first American many of my students have ever met off of a screen, and I try to alleviate the imperial nature of my country of birth by attempting to understand the lives of those in my classroom.

I have seen eyes dulled by grief, war, state-sponsored medication or even self-induced stupor courtesy of the illegal hash market. My students often — the young ones always — roll up to class with the saccharine-smelling energy drinks that they use to wake up every morning. Many have been in the "system" — meaning that they have a case worker involved, and sometimes take medication. Some have sported ankle bracelets, hijabs, designer handbags, even surgical augmentations. Some have not fallen within the gender polarity that our culture insists on. This is the system built for those who do not fare well in the traditional education system, offering a last chance to possibly get on board a life of normalcy, whatever that means. The dream, if you were to listen to Danish politicians, is integration — although not in the truest sense of the word, but in the way that *you* become *us*, because we are *better* and the only reason we feel this is because, obviously, we don't *know* better. Rarely will you ever meet a Westerner who truly knows how indebted we ought to be to the academic excellence that comes out of certain regions of the world other than ours.

I had washed ashore on a centuries-old war and found myself in the middle of a conflict that went back even further than I could have ever imagined and which had, for better or for worse, shaped the geographies of the region I now found myself in and even the world. Sometimes the war was with the Christian, sometimes with the "Saracen", the Jew, the woman, the refugee — the other.

When one looks closer at the details, one can detect patterns of expulsion and displacement, and sometimes even of extermination. Through the dispossession of land, the expulsion of people, the torture of those who do not fall in line, what was once a localized oppression radiates out into the world in the form of concentration camps, built by Europeans, even on African soil.

And I suppose this is where the biggest of my discomforts lay in teaching — pushing this idea, whether consciously or subconsciously, that one culture is superior to another. One could say that my experiences as a Black woman in the education system has made me sensitive to this, but I don't think "sensitive" is the word; I would suggest the word "weary." It's maddening to participate in anything in which you do not see yourself — it's a particular kind of violence, even.

In a work culture that is about the grind, I've had to step back to ascertain the lifestyle that suits me best and create it. Teaching in Denmark had exacerbated my already frazzled nerves. Although the travel involved in my book tour could sometimes feel unsettling, at least I could move at my own pace during it and not get caught up in the hustle and bustle of modern living, which, the older I get, seems to grow more challenging to keep up with. Not that I would want to. If there's one thing I have learned in the past few years of my life it's that I do enjoy my own company. I enjoy having the freedom to be. "Freedom is the ability to use your time in any way that you desire," the poet and musician Gil Scott-Heron once wisely said.

There have to be other ways of living. By this time in my life, although I shared an apartment with someone, I realized that the traditional domestic setup wasn't for me. The truth is that I was happiest in a living situation when I lived at Flux, which had over twenty people living there at some point. I enjoyed living collectively. Flux was a collective on Kent Avenue back when Williamsburg was full of artists, students and the working class. Flux, founded by some of my former college classmates — including the writers Morgan Meis and Stephanie Anne Goldberg, bassist-turned-botanist Toshi Yano and all-around talent Jason Smalls, among others — was an eclectic mix of artists, musicians and writers from all over the globe — Japan, Portugal, Denmark, Germany, the Caribbean and throughout the united settler states. We occupied a warehouse that once existed on the corner of Kent and Metropolitan, an off-white, two-floor building that had been a feather factory during that neighborhood's industrial heyday.

And, like Fukuoka, my job had taken a toll on me emotionally. As previously mentioned, many of my students in Denmark were casualties of the wars we in the west instigated. Whether it was the many wars in Iraq and Afghanistan or the conditions we created in so many other countries — I met them all in my classroom. Young men, the same age as my son, who had walked the perilous journey from Afghanistan, had often lost everything — including their families — on this journey. Many had to hand over their valuables in a practice that the Nazis once used. There are detention centers full of the desperate, fenced away, away from the Danes' notice, whose lives will be a series of days and nights cut off from the society in which they have found themselves. There are children there, and many will face forced return to their countries of origin, despite evidence of the dangers. Our borders are violent: there is murder at our borders. Humans are trafficked at our borders. Children disappear.

Here is a record of an attempted escape from teaching, of a journey of crossing borders, seeking refuge, health, *marronage*, that I embarked upon to find home...

Part One

1.

Agatha Christie is a fucking racist 2016[1]

"So what are you saying? That we're racist?" he asked as he looks frantically around the room for evidence to the contrary. And indeed, as if by magic, he seemed to have found it: "We're not racist," he said, staring at me squarely in the eye. "There's a little Asian girl in the fourth grade." And as if he too realized how silly that sounded, he then tried to appear as if he was tidying up his already bare desk. It was all rather comical, really — his office was meant to effuse authority and the *norm* — the framed family picture that didn't reveal the son's tormented boarding-school soul or wife's disappointment that they had ended up in Denmark as opposed to some former colonial country where it wouldn't be frowned upon to have cheap, colored help, unlike in this Scandinavian socialist shithole of a place that almost made domestic help prohibitive! Thankfully, she had her ways! And further behind him, on the wall, was a row of portraits — serious-faced former principals who all bore expressions one would more expect from prison wardens than leaders of a school for children.

---

1   Now, I'm not really saying she's a racist…I'm just saying that there was a book, written by said person, with the name, *Ten Little N*ggers*. Ahem.

Did my boss really just say that?

How could I have been stupid enough to get into a conversation about race with Matthew Saunders, the principal of the Copenhagen School, one of the most (if not *the* most) prestigious schools in the Kingdom of Denmark? I really should have known better. And should have been more prepared, too.

I had known about the school even before I arrived. Many famous Danish people sent their children there (I was told) — there was even evidence of that troublesome relic from the past: royalty.

At the time, I was still dabbling with the absurd notion that I could fit into the norm — whatever that's supposed to mean. The capitalist, neo-liberal devil on one shoulder whispered, *It will look good on your resumé.* My ancestors, on the other, said, *Really?!* But the capitalist, neo-liberal devil knew that I had rent to pay.

I suppose it would look good on my resumé, I sighed as I studied the school's ivy edifice before entering to interview with the principal. Looking back, I even felt a little honored to have been invited to interview here. It was a prestigious and obviously exclusive school, and although I knew that there was no way I could last there, I was curious. However, I hadn't expected my downfall to be so easy.

It's not that I personally value elitism and exclusivity — but alas! I was forced out into this capitalist, elitist, sexist, classist, heteronormative world from the comforts of my mother's womb. And forced out I was. "They had to induce labor with you!" my mother would tell me, over and over again, as a child growing up. "You didn't want to come out!" And she'd cackle and double over with laughter. And now I understand. I was smart: I knew what was out there, beyond the walls of my mother's womb, from out between the curtains of her labia, perhaps the only true home I have ever had. And now, here I am, in Matthew Saunders's office no less, having the dreaded "R" discussion.

When I had first been invited to interview at the school, I had thought it meant they had recognized my talents as a teacher and wanted me as part of the team. And I liked the small school in the middle of Copenhagen immediately upon arriving — the elementary school classes were designed to look like the classrooms of yesteryear — with inkwells on wooden desks that I imagined made some of the parents feel as though they were dropping their little ones off at a provincial school in France.

Yes, it was stuffy in that upper-middle-class way, but it was a job. And to be honest, ever since I realized that I was going to be a writer, at the tender age of three, I've approached every opportunity I've had as writing material. What's that saying? "Beware of writers. They mix with all classes of society and are therefore the most dangerous?" From losing my virginity to all the various jobs I've had in my lifetime — every experience I have is up for grabs. And there was writing material written all over this place: the British principal who went to Oxford; the mesmerizing effect this seemed to have on the mostly Danish staff. "He went to school with the guys from Monty Python!" All the middle-aged teachers, it seemed, would swoon.

I had been recommended by a former colleague of mine, someone I had worked with at another exclusive school years before. Camille Cox was originally from England and worked as a primary school teacher. She was warm and engaging, and her classroom, much to my delight, resembled a jungle. She always packed healthy lunches, and whenever I saw her she greeted me with kindness. Camille was one of those people who didn't really honor personal space, but I'd let her get away with it because she only emitted goodness. There wasn't a bad bone in her body.

But then they fired her after twenty years of service.

It was this expulsion that left me with a sour taste in my mouth for the type of environment some schools choose to cultivate. Camille had been forced out of her job by her colleagues, and I had a front-row seat to this witch burning. I saw the meetings, the tears, the gradual breaking down that corporate environments resort to when they have decided that someone isn't in line with their brand.

"She doesn't fit our profile," the principal explained to me one day when I had asked. *Oh yeah?* I remember thinking. *I wonder how long till you figure out that I don't, either.*

I couldn't understand how her former colleagues had all seemed to turn on her the way that they had. It seemed unnecessarily cruel. They were, in essence, not only taking away her job, which from all evidence she was passionate about; they were hell-bent on breaking her soul. If it was traumatic for me to watch, I had no idea what she was going through. And it wasn't even necessarily that the other staff were evil — there was something about that place that always interested me. It was this: I have worked in many different schools, and I couldn't help but notice that despite the swanky facilities of the school, there was a general malaise among the teachers. Individually, they were great, but collectively, the way that the school was structured — it was something else, as I was witnessing. It was the first time I had worked in a school where the hierarchy was so obvious: the principals and director were all British. The teachers, who came from all over the world, were always usually middle class or striving to be.

One day, an English colleague of mine, privy to the thorny issue of the British caste system, enlightened me. "Camille is from a council estate," the handsome Welsh teacher told me. I liked Mr. Davies — he always gave me a laugh by explaining to me the ins and outs of British culture.

"What?"

"She's from a council estate, government housing," he explained, "and the rest," he looked over his shoulder in an exaggerated William Shatner kind of way to make sure no one could hear, "are all a bunch of upper-class wannabes. And that guy over there" — I follow his finger to see him pointing at the director of the school — "he's what we call a toff — an upper-class twit."

I made it a point to remain in contact with Camille, who thankfully found a place that seemed to appreciate her. Years later, when she needed to take some time off, she recommended me for the job.

I was received warmly by the teachers, who all greeted me with an amused expression on their faces, principal included. The students and staff alike would meet in the courtyard between buildings every morning to hear Mr. Saunders, the principal who spoke not a word of Danish but who the parents had hoped would inculcate their children with "proper" English — meaning only the upper-class British accent allowed, no American! *Clever*, I thought. *So this is what some upper-class Brits do — the empire may be hidden, but not in our school systems*. Watch the Oxford graduate attract large salaries heading international schools that turn to Britain's shitty scholastic standards, which do nothing more than reproduce hierarchical and oppressive societies. Ah, Europe.

The birthplace of genocide and fascism. How else to continue a system?

Mr. Saunders had seemed to like me on the spot — in fact, he offered me the job right then and there. I do remember seeing a shadow of suspicion cross his eyes when he commented on my resumé. "A degree in race and representation?" He cocked his eyebrow at me as if he were a cop informing me of how many miles I was driving over the speed limit.

"Oh, that—" I had learned to tone down any talk about race in Denmark. And I was, of course, doing a horrible job at it. These talks only led to quickened heartbeats and my wanting to bash the person's head in for the apparent reluctance they were showing toward, god forbid, having to tread in another's shoes. Despite the name of my degree, the truth is that nothing could have prepared me for the culture shock of moving to what my friend Miriam calls *Scandimania*. It really did feel as if I was in a Nella Larsen novel, because quicksand would be an appropriate metaphor.

"What you going over there for?" my now deceased father had asked me so many moons ago, when I had first told him that I was moving to Northern Europe. "Stay here; Europe is no place for Black people," he said, saying in essence what the Dali Lama would say years later, although with different words.

We were both sitting in his small, single-occupancy room — the television emitting a daytime game show. There was a young mother down the hall, her young son running ecstatically up and down the common hall that they shared, his mouth making as if he was a car. My father's room was in the basement. Slivers of sunlight danced across his linoleum floor. He was seated on a shaky kitchen chair and shifted his legs further apart. I understood why his friends called him "chief" — he was quiet but always in command, and no matter what he wore, he stood out. It was a combination of his dark copper-brown skin and the way his face defied convention. His eyes looked Asian, his body and gait recalled the lush jungles of our homeland, where I imagined he belonged. But it wasn't even about his features — his strength and pride said this. His slender fingers, with perfect fingertips, could fix anything in the home — including electronic appliances and even his own Hammond B3. His Afro was perfectly round, his smile soft. My father's very existence, like so many of the Global majority, challenged the absurdity of European supremacy.

But the truth was, to paraphrase Stuart Hall, maybe I moved to Northern Europe because I needed to get away from my family. I know it sounds harsh, and let me be clear: I don't think my family is any worse than any other. But sometimes, in order to grow, you have to make that leap. And at least in Denmark I have an excuse for feeling out of place: I am foreign. And I was determined not to lose joy to the Danes' (to me) peculiar ways of life: the religious fervor with which they approach the eating of open sandwiches or hoist their strawberry-and-cream colored flag.

Sure, Denmark has a race problem — ranging from intentional national amnesia about its colonial past to the insistence that it *did not have a race problem*; this was what propelled me to begin blogging in 2005. *Blackgirl on Mars: Notes on a Life in Copenhagen (or how my alienation brings me closer to people)* was one of the first blogs to examine race in the blogosphere, particularly in Northern Europe.

But to be fair (no pun intended), where in the world isn't there a race problem? For wherever Europe went, she took her only original idea: race and its offspring, racism. If I was going to have to survive in what the gone-too-soon Danish-Palestinian poet Yahya Hassan once called "Eurocentric Fundamentalism," then I needed to do some fieldwork. And there can be no better place than the motherland of White people. In this delusional space, fed by late-night readings of St. Baldwin, I had begun to fashion myself as some kind of white-people whisperer.

In Denmark, there were the constant, cyclical, summer editorials on the latest product that suddenly became hip to the idea that having a candy called "n*gger kisses" just wasn't going to cut it. The trolls would come out of the woodwork and debates would be had with folks who complained, "Why do we have to be so politically correct?!" In response to which I would think to myself, "What's so wrong with being considerate?! Seriously!" It was as if the racism I felt I had fled in the States had followed me, except that here, where the very invention of race occurred, they now claim it doesn't exist! The general idea is that racism did not happen here, that it was a distinctly American thing — like, where do you think White Americans came from? From outer space?

All of these, however, were themes that I would air out on my blog, realizing very quickly that I would need to have an outlet for all of the thousand-cut grievances I was finding I would have to navigate in the coziest and happiest country in the world.

I laughed at the irony that my father had warned me about moving here and I had replied, so naively at the time, "But it's Europe! They're more progressive!"

"Yeah, right," my father had answered, taking a sip of his tepid beer. "What someone who loves Marcus Garvey doing going over to the White man's country?" he asked me, his eyes bemused.

The truth is that, at that time, I had convinced myself I wasn't going to let myself get uptight over racial matters anymore, which, if you know me, is an incredibly ridiculous idea. By the time my father and I were having this conversation, the truth was that I wanted to run away from anything that had to do with race. And when I had visited Denmark the summer before, I felt an ease in my body that I had been unable to feel in both Trinidad and Brooklyn. In the Denmark that I had visited, the visceral nature of racism was tucked away, barely perceptible in the light of its inhabitants' Danish designer lamps. I was tired. And I had hoped that there would be some relief thousands of miles away from these "united" settler States. I too would become a settler, amidst Denmark's eternal struggle towards its own identity. "Am I an ethnostate?" it asks itself every election year.

Sure, I could have returned to the island of my parents' birth — Trinidad and Tobago — or gone anywhere else for that matter (a Black country, maybe?). Trinidad and Tobago was out of the question at that point, although I would continue to visit over the years because I had felt too confined.

I had considered Uganda and even visited the consulate's office in New York, but as soon as I found out I had to take vaccines and apply for visas, my ADHD set in and my eyes became heavy with sleep. I needed to be able to just get on a plane.

And as much as I hate to admit it, as stupid as it makes me feel as I type this — I had somehow fallen for the idea of "progressive Europe". Despite how much I had invested in reading and studying Black history, my precious consciousness had already been imprinted upon in school. For even though I would always go to mostly Black schools, the curriculum was rarely ever designed for us. My schooling only further promoted Eurocentric fundamentalism, even if my teachers were not White. There were stellar exceptions, of course, like Ms. Joan Kissoon, my secondary school history teacher in Trinidad.

Ms. Kissoon wore silky, frilly blouses and colorful slacks. She wore her jet-black hair cut short and, at the time, smoked cigarettes. Her rouge was too pink for her brown skin, but it was the Eighties, so maybe it was the style. She lived in Santa Cruz, which I thought was cool because Santa Cruz is this beautiful mountain village that my grandmother's family is from. At the time, she used swear words in class, which for us Form 1 students at this Catholic secondary school run by nuns was the greatest rebellion you could enact.

Let me take you back to that tropical classroom in the early Eighties. It's a beautiful, sunny afternoon, and I'm sitting in my Form 1 class, which has corridors on either side: one for the teachers, the other for the students, and both for the breeze. Right outside the louvered windows to my left is the private Belmont road that goes further up the hill, among the trees and bushes, to our court, where the children of the upper echelons practice field hockey, tennis and badminton; the others, mostly Black girls, like me, play netball.

I'm slouched over my wood desk — a bench with a desk that opens and closes. I notice how the sunlight dances off the leaves of the trees up on the hills right outside the open door. There's about twenty of us in the classroom, and it's after lunch, so we've all got our heads on the desks. I'm twelve years old; it's already been two years since I moved to Trinidad from Brooklyn. This Catholic school in Belmont was unlike anything I had ever experienced in my young life, and

I really liked it: girls only, school uniforms and a pretty decent curriculum.

In walks Ms. Kissoon, her gait energetic, her brown hands in the pockets of her well-creased slacks. "Good afternoon, Ms. Kissoon," we all say as we slowly stand to greet her and slump back into our wooden benches as if even the weight of our own bodies is too much to bear in this hot weather. The heat is killer, and it will not be the first time I wonder about the sense of wearing polyester in the Caribbean heat.

"Good afternoon, class!" Ms. Kissoon says, a smile dancing on her otherwise serious face. She places the small stack of copybooks that she's been carrying in the crook of her arm onto the desk, which she then leans against as she asks us to take out our history books. I really like the textbook that we've been studying from, appreciating that the narrative seems to be more about us telling our own history as opposed to someone else telling it to us. It is true that we have inherited a lot of our culture from our previous colonial thieves, but that would only seem to be the case for those who don't know what they are seeing.

"Where were we?" Ms. Kissoon flips through her textbook as the rest of us do the same. The fan that sits on the desk blows warm air. I found the chapter we were last reading and read the title out loud, "The Mercantile System."

"Okay," Ms. Kissoon says. "So I see we've already covered how the White man came from Europe, murdered the Indigenous people wherever they went, stole their land, went to Africa, did the same thing, except this time they take a few of us. And did they stop there? No, of course not; then they went to India." We giggle.

"Allyuh know how it is…" She begins to draw with her chalk on the blackboard. "This is Europe; this is the Caribbean —

people minding they own business over here in Africa, people minding they own business over here in India, people minding they own business. But Europe? They in all a we business." And we all give a laugh that many of us inherit: the right to laugh. It is the laugh that emerges when you find yourself living in the shadow of colonialism, a space that gains you access to the fact that the emperor has always been and always will be stark-fucking-naked. We are born knowing that Europe and her culture are hypocrites.

What I should have done before moving to Denmark was commune with ancestor Baldwin. "Don't do it," he would have said in his gravelly voice, legs crossed, cigarette dangling between his elegant fingers. "Just don't do it. Stay here. Do your work here." He looks at me with those big, intense eyes of his and passes the cigarette to me. I admire his beautiful brown face, the face that seemed etched with pathways to liberation. But alas, I had no such communion.

And home — if our biology is our biography, then I could pull continents together again as if I was some walking Pangea, bloodlines clashing together like Gondwana and Laurasia. Every stone is a pillow, every place a bed, is my motto. Besides, it's not my fault I was forced out of my mother's vajayjay to navigate a world that had been so hell-bent on restricting the movement of folks who look like me; a world run by people who, according to ancestor bell hooks, base their very value, built their very riches, on the devaluation of all life. Travel is my protest: whenever I feel stuck, I buy a plane ticket.

I had thought my father's focus and ideology old-fashioned, that the world was perhaps, now, post-racial — in the Nineties! I laughed bitterly at myself. It wasn't the reality. It was me trying to bend my own reality so that life wouldn't be so painful.

But back in the office, sitting across from my British boss, none of these memories could help me now. "Well, no, see, this is what happened…" I stumbled, angry at myself that I couldn't seem to take a moment to get my thoughts straight. I did indeed snap in the classroom. I could see that that was not good but everything seemed to take such a nosedive so quickly.

As far as jobs went, I did actually enjoy teaching at this school. The students, for the most part, were all likable and, well, kids. Every now and then, of course, I'd get a student who didn't really do much and let me know through their eyes that they thought I was a loser, you know, like the help, as you see their father was the CEO of blah blah blah. Well, actually, they would even say it to my face, but for the most part the students were cool and diligent; there to learn, excel and then move on to the next level of their lives, which probably would include guaranteed employment in the upper echelons of society, a zealous belief in the Danish state's ability to fix everything (including one's mental health) and, for many of them, alcohol.

Once, I had given this same class a homework assignment. We had just read a short story about someone who had been granted three wishes. "If you could get three wishes," I asked, "what would they be?" Some of the answers were the usual, like having more wishes or the newest video game console, superpowers even, but many, about half of the students, wanted "to be rich." The Scandinavian angled-cut clothes many of the students wore didn't denote financial insecurity. On the contrary. Yet here they were, over half the class, wanting to be rich.

"Why not just change the economic system?" I had asked, curious why it wasn't mentioned as a wish. They stared back at me as if I had lifted my skirt and flashed my ass. So much for the classroom being a place of radical dreaming. I of course explained what I meant, which became a lesson about different economic models. But they all looked at me, their blue and brown eyes clouded over with suspicion, when I mentioned concepts such as universal income, housing, and all of my other radical ideas of inclusivity and access for all.

Let's get back to the book. Well, there were several, but there was one particular one. Each student had to bring in an English book of their choice to show me so that I could make a note of it. The idea was that, at the end of the semester, each student would hand in a book report. As we sat in the classroom, with its disheveled bookcases and crooked posters of classroom values that included slogans such as "tolerance" and "community," the students worked independently on an assignment while I called each of them up, one by one, so that they could show me their book of choice, which I carefully noted. It was one of those moments in labor when one's consciousness and actions are one; a slight feeling of self-importance filled me up. It was a bit Kafkaesque. The books offered seemed to reflect their parents' reading tastes for the most part — a deluge of Paul Auster (yawn) and the *Twilight* and *Harry Potter* series. Others surprised me — one even brought up a copy of *The White Boy Shuffle*. Now that is what I'm talking about. I smiled as I noted the title and returned it to the blond boy, whose eyes seemed to give me a Black Power fist in the air. And that's why I stayed — for the kids who were truly hungry for something different, for different ways of doing things, seeing things, learning and thinking about things. Scandimania's homogeneity created nooses around children and anyone else who didn't fit into this "norm." I know; I saw them every day as a teacher.

The students all worked as the winter's day ripened and then waned into darkness outside the school's windows. Aside from the sound of music coming from some of the students' headphones, the classroom was quiet but very busy.

And then it appeared, as if some Dickensian ghost taunting me: *Ten Little N*ggers* by Agatha Christie. As I read the title, my eyes searched the cover, frantic to find some meaning. There was a golliwog hanging from the ceiling of a porch and blood splattered all over the banister right behind it. Behind was a tree, an iguana and then the ocean. It looked very MK-Ultra, BBC even. For my all non-British readers, golliwogs, as I had learned as a child in Trinidad from an Enid Blyton book, were the British Empire's way of dehumanizing her Black British subjects. According to the *New Oxford American Dictionary* a golliwog is a "soft doll with bright clothes, a black face and fuzzy hair." But this definition belies its racist nature. It's a stereotypical depiction of Black people. Eurocentric fundamentalism is such a tenuous condition one could argue billions of dollars must be used to uphold to keep the global majority in our places. Was this some kind of joke? I looked up hastily at the student who had brought the book to my desk, and he looked down, his gaze avoiding mine. I knew the student — he was the son of a teacher here. Suddenly, a memory came back to me in the split of a millisecond:

Back when I had first started, I sat grading papers in the teachers' room — a large room that had several desks where we, the teachers, could grab a coffee, catch up on work or even talk. There was only one other person in the staffroom, a tall, lanky man who was around his late forties. There was something about the way he approached me — with a familiarity that was inappropriate — that I found annoying. But I was new and braced myself for the small conversations I would have to have with my new colleagues. Most of them were pleasant, accommodating even, willing to explain things like how to get to the library, which was through an entirely different staircase from the main building, and that you should never dare to go anywhere without your keys because you might find yourself all the way on the top floor of the library with no keys and no way to get in, as the door to the library was actually behind this door — simple things like that. But race?

There was this other teacher, the history teacher I had met previously, a small Danish man who seemed pleasantly surprised to see me and who took it upon himself to tell me that it was he who had written the Danish history books that many Danish students would read throughout the country. He flipped through a copy of his hardcover textbook to show me how many pages he had dedicated to Denmark's foray into the business of Caribbean plantations and African West Coast fortresses — in other words, the trafficking and enslavement of thousands of human beings. This was also a little annoying.

Once I did a "Colonial Copenhagen" tour with a group of Danish eighth graders. They were engaged and interested. I broke them into groups and had them find certain buildings that were connected to Denmark's colonial past. There were at least ten structures in Copenhagen associated with the trade in enslaved Africans, including the statue of King Frederik V at Amalienborg Palace, the king who got Denmark involved in the first place, which was gifted to him by the Asiatic Company, which made its money in the trade. There's the West Indian Warehouse on the harbor — the proposed site of the *I Am Queen Mary* statue — which was once owned by traders in enslaved Africans, the West India Trading Company. Denmark colonized what is now called the US Virgin Islands from 1672 to 1917, and its merchants were involved in the so-called triangular trade from the 1670s until the 1840s. The students, even the surly ones, became animated, interested. "They don't teach us this," one student said, "but they should."

By the point the lanky teacher had sauntered up to me, I had been in Denmark for many years, and I was wary. This wasn't even a week before the episode with his son took place in my classroom full of seventh graders, who all seemed to wait with baited breath.

The father. He had a weird vibe about him. He had asked me about myself and had managed to mention that he was familiar with my blog in a disapproving way. At the time, I had brushed the incident off and just kept moving, making a pact with myself to avoid him at all costs. It wasn't something I could explain to my boss, either. Most White people will just call you paranoid. And to make matters even more complicated, I wasn't even the one to say the book was racist. It was actually another student, a young blond boy whose long bangs always fell over his blue, troubled eyes. Out of all the students in the class, he was by far the most mouthy, and to be honest, I kind of liked him because he was so irritating. I always like troublemakers. I could tell he was going through a lot, which was why he was acting the way he was, and I tried to support him the best way that I could, with patience.

He had recently moved back to Denmark after living some years in Brooklyn, New York. I had also learned he was a person of interest in the school because Mr. Saunders always seemed in a rush to ask about how well he was faring in my class, something I had never suspected anything about until now.

When I told the students that I was originally from Brooklyn, this student volunteered that he had lived there. Later, the principal told me that he was having a difficult time returning to Denmark and settling back into Danish society.

It was this student who had blurted, "This school is so racist! You all are so racist! Who brings a book like that to school?! I hate it here!" There was so much pain in his voice.

I was trying to damage control, and he wasn't helping! This is exactly the kind of thing I wanted to avoid. That damn teacher! His son stood there with a smirk on his face. It revealed everything. This young boy was being conditioned to be a bully, at the least, and his parents weren't helping.

"Good, good," my boss now has the nerve to look me in the eyes. "There's not a racist person in this school, here, Lesley-Ann. As you can see."

"Yes, Mr. Saunders," I replied dryly, rolling my eyes into my forehead.

I wanted to suggest to the principal that it was an opportunity for the class, even the school, to get involved in a conversation about race. But I grew exhausted by the idea when I remembered the grammar book that was in use. It was all about a drug dealer named Leroy in LA. At the time, many Danish students were using a grammar book that employed stories of drug sales and prostitution in the US to learn proper sentence construction. I tried to complain: a) because of the content — it was very violent and sexually explicit — and b) because it was racist as hell.

"But where does it say their race?" My principal, exasperated, had asked me.

Bitch, his name is Leroy.

And to be fair, I really didn't have the energy, or the tools, to take on this project with a leader who, although it seemed as if he wanted to have a discussion, already had his preconceived idea as to where the conversation should go. Besides, I'm not Fannie Lou Hamer. Shit like this made me understand why Queen Mary burned it all down. Too bad she didn't do it here.

The class had erupted after the boy yelled charges of racism, and in an effort to get him to quiet down, I had ordered him out of the room. He had gone home, upset, and this is the situation the principal seemed most interested in. "But Christian, he went home?"

"Yes. He was very upset. But he didn't do anything wrong — he spoke out of turn — but he didn't do anything, really—"

"Did he have permission to go home?"

"Well, no, but... again, he didn't do anything wrong." I felt uneasy about the focus on the boy as if he was solely to blame for the disruption in the classroom.

"Well, I'll talk to the boy who brought the book in. I mean, he couldn't have known, obviously," he said while he busied himself at his desk. "I mean, his father teaches here... words change all the time... it's hard to keep up." I realized that the school had wanted to get rid of this student from Brooklyn and this was their excuse.

"That boy. He's trouble. He had a hard time in Brooklyn. Got beat up by all the Black kids. He's messed up in the head." This student was obviously experiencing a lot of change, and he needed the school's support, not punishment. I couldn't escape the fact that, no matter what school I worked in, there was always such a level of violence used toward certain children and teachers, like this student and Camille Cox.

"No, he's not, Mr. Saunders. He's not messed up in the head. He understands a lot of things. He needs our support, not our abandonment."

"That will be all, Lesley-Ann. Thank you." And Mr. Saunders directed me to his door with his eyes. Shit. *I'm not going to last here*, I realized as I walked slowly and dejectedly from the office of shiny oak trimmings and impressive portraits of previous principals whose years there ensured that the school continued its tradition of White ignorance.

2.

"God creates, Europe destroys" — Linnaeus[2]

Throughout the years, my blog would attract all sorts of attention: from women who mistook my experiences to mean that I was advocating for the swirl community (le sigh — it's not that I'm against interracial dating, obviously, but why do folks have to make it a thing?!), to others who were considering moving to Denmark and were interested in reading about my experiences, as well as other bloggers and writers. I was mostly a grumpy, melancholic expat in Scandimania — my blog protested neoliberalism, it didn't embrace it. And then there were folks living here, in Denmark, who also began to read my work. By this time I had also already begun to perform my poetry publicly and engage with the artist community. Suddenly I was being invited to things and thus began my third — albeit just as a short foray — into activism.

The first was when I volunteered at the War Resisters League as a high school student. I would go to the Macy's Thanksgiving Day Parade and hand out "Don't buy war toys" flyers along with a team of other student volunteers and WRL staff to kick the Reserve Officers' Training Corp out of

2   Okay, Linnaeus *did not* write that! What he did say was, "God creates, Linneaus organizes."

poor and Black high schools. My own mostly Black, Puerto Rican and Chinese Manhattan high school had gotten metal detectors around the same time, and I wish I had understood and connected the violence of that to my activism.

The second time I veered into the world of activism was when I ran for the position of School Secretary when I was a Sophomore at said high school. My campaign promise, to have music in the cafeteria, was delivered once I had won.

Here in Denmark, I participated in a few panels, debates and events. It was the early days, when folks were all coming out, meeting each other and offering each other support. I even organized some of these events myself, but found that I had to step back as my health — emotional and physical — was not balanced. My nervous system was dysregulated. Besides having a full schedule of teaching, my son was still a child. I had experienced that whenever I did too much, wore myself thin, he would suffer my impatience. I didn't want to do that to him.

I also was uncomfortable with the role folks seemed to want to project onto me. From all appearances, I had been doing well: I had my own apartment, and I was never afraid to speak up. But I don't believe in leadership — and I felt many times that I was being asked to lead and organize. The activism milieu at the time was also a mixed bag, full of folks who advocated for real, fundamental change, and others who merely wanted access to the material gains that they felt were denied them. I've been happy to see how many others have continued the work, however, and some of them I consider friends.

Because I have very little experience in activism, it took me years to understand that some folks' idea of liberation has a very corporate structure, with heroes and all. And full disclosure: I'm just not into corporations. I don't like the culture, and

I don't like what it mostly seems to bring out in people. My first experience of corporate life was at the children's book publishing company Scholastic, located in trendy downtown Manhattan. I had just graduated from college and wanted to continue in publishing. This is the same publishing company that, years later, published *A Birthday Cake for George Washington* — you know, the first US president, who used dentures made from the teeth of enslaved Africans? Scholastic actually thought that publishing a book about the enslaved Hercules and his daughter baking a cake for George Washington was a good idea. I wasn't surprised. In the first and only job I have ever been fired from, my now former boss had suggested that I get a job in a store.

So I stepped back from activism. I decided to focus on my health. I decided to focus on those things that brought me joy. That filled me up and gave me life. And on this journey, I made an interesting discovery: I found that some of the most amazing teachers weren't human at all. I allowed my interest to lead me and discovered that not only were plants capable teachers, but that they would prove to be integral in my healing process.

I decided to go to plant school. It's not a physical school with humans as teachers, and I don't sit at any one desk. This plant school is not the one where you buy lots of cute baby plants, either. It's not a course where I will finish and get a certificate — but it is one in which I have become a humble student. And plants, they are my teachers. This school gives me support in ways that no human has ever been able to do. Throughout the years, I have found that engaging with plants helps keep my stress levels down and is a great way for me to metabolize many of the experiences I find myself having. It made complete sense to me when I learned in *Braiding*

Sweetgrass that the various native names for plants are usually some version of "those who take care of us."

I've even incorporated plants into my classrooms and teaching. Together with some of my students I've grown beans in cups and worked with local parks to assist in their gardens. I know that when we do this, we become a little more aware of the other life forms on our planet. And that's a lesson I definitely want to impart.

Without sounding mushy, it helps me maintain my perspective when I think of the fact that none of us would be here without plants, which showed up on our planet around three hundred thousand years ago. When I stop and ponder the beauty of a plant, when I stop to ponder all that we owe the plant kingdom, it helps take me away from the pain of racism; until I encountered the work of Carl Linnaeus — because in Europe, quiet as it's kept, everything is about race.

My lifelong respect for and curiosity about plants can be traced back to my earliest memories in Trinidad of working in the garden with my grandmother. On this small patch of land that surrounded our squat, gray house, which was separated from the sidewalk and road by a rusty, white iron gate, I learned about the land and the relationship we could forge with it. Through the various plants my grandmother, Mummy Hildred, cultivated — like hot peppers grown from seed or the ruby-red sorrel harvested for another Christmas — this mysterious and fascinating world was revealed to me, a world that seemed to operate outside the laws of humans, including our construct of linear time.

Whenever I look at an emerging leaf, I am always struck by its perfection: the cell structure, patterns and color. What is this world that I live so close to but know so little about?

That my grandmother's name is Hildred is also telling. It was something my curious mind had to ask her about when I was a child, already knowing the name to be uncommon, at least in our part of the world.

"Well, it was during the war," she tells me while digging up some dirt to plant a flamboyant sapling in our yard. "They had wanted to name me Hildegard, but my family thought it sounded too German. So Hildred it is." I've since looked a bit into the life of Hildegard of Bingen, and was not disappointed. She believed the only sin in life was to "dry up." She believed that we were all capable of healing.

According to Matthew Fox, author of *Hildegard of Bingen: A Saint for Our Times: Unleashing Her Power in the 21st Century*, she was placed in the care of the Jutta monastery, she was a thinker, scientist, musician and architect, among other talents. She was into healing herbs, stones and crystals, and left many insights regarding plants, animals and diet. She believed in the erotic nature of life, and that this is our divine right. After the death of Jutta, she was the abbess in search of whom women flooded the monastery, donating enough dowries to build two monasteries for this growing community of spiritual women who eschewed marriage. A believer in the cosmic Christ, she continued the Celtic tradition of relating to earth as a living organism, and believed in the deep wisdom of the feminine. For her, god was in everything — everything was god. She believed in *veriditas* — greening power, the color of the heart chakra, the color of love. Just to be alive is erotic in nature, and our senses are our divine right. She believed that if we destroy the rest of creation, creation will destroy humanity. She knew that we were part of the web of life and that the earth must not be destroyed. You have to do something that will get you wet and green and moist and juicy, like the earth recently rained upon; the petrichor erupts, unleashing our connections to it all.

I don't think that there could have been a better namesake for my grandmother, who, although contained by Catholicism, had the classic wild-woman archetype dancing behind her eyes, which would often make my grandfather lament, "You see you? It's a good thing you never got an education. I would be in trouble for sure!"

Plants have always played a role in my healing, whether it was taking bush tea to alleviate fever or learning that the original aspirin comes from the bark of the willow tree, not the German company, and that it has been in use for more than 3500 years. The active agent, salicin, is what helps with general pain relief and is considered an antipyretic.

When you delve into the world of plants, one of the first things you'll probably encounter is the way that plants are named and categorized: the taxonomy. And you cannot learn about taxonomy without hearing the name Carl Linnaeus — the father of taxonomy.

It was the South Korean-Danish performance artist Yong Sun Gullach who, one day, broke it all down for me. "Linnaeus was the one, or at least one of the first, to depict a racial hierarchy– stratification system, attributing certain racial stereotypes based on ideas of race." Yong Sun, a Korean adoptee, uses performance to challenge the dominant narrative around Western adoptions. Throughout her work, she questions the Good Samaritan/savior image that is promoted when it comes to Western (mostly White) adoptive parents of (mostly) non-White children. Her work makes the connections between demand, exploitation and supply when it comes to transnational adoption policies, highlighting the ways in which gender, class and race play into them and how this trafficking of babies even helped rebuild South Korea. I also learned through her and the Forum for Adoption Politics, a group committed to offering support to adoptees, that the Black babies born to German women during the war were the beginning of transnational adoption.

It is through my newfound obsession with plants that I stumbled upon Linnaeus's name again. Here in Denmark, I have begun to collect tropical plants. I know I do this as much to help me feel a little bit more at home as to learn. You eventually read that the weeping fig you bought from Ikea twenty-two years ago while you were pregnant, and which is still alive (albeit with much fewer leaves), is called *Ficus benjamina*, and that this way of classifying, using these two descriptors, is known as binomial nomenclature — which is a direct result of Linnaeus's legacy. So, in this way, my calathea is a *Calathea ornata*, and my angel wing begonia is a *Begonia coccinea*. This system of categorizing is implicitly hierarchical.

When I read about Linnaeus, it is easy for me to get swept away by the details of his story: a poor boy from southern Sweden whose father's passion for plants fueled his. It is the story of a little boy who had his first garden when he was just five years old. Who was terrorized in a school that practiced corporal punishment and was, in fact, a poor student. The story of a young man who got lost in the world of plants and whose observations of that world would lay much of the foundation for natural science. This was in the 1700s, during the height of Europe's colonial period and "Enlightenment" — that period when Europe humanized herself at the expense of the entire planet and everything else on her. While this Swedish man attempted to bring order to this world's creations, Europe herself was going through a massive "discovery" of worlds whose inhabitants were as foreign to Europeans as Europeans were to them. In a way, Linnaeus could be viewed as Europe itself: Where would we be without the European compulsion to name and organize? Perhaps in a more peaceful, prosperous and equal place? I'm just asking. We are a culture that often uses nouns for concepts that used to be expressed as verbs, thereby halting the dynamism of existence, bounding it into seemingly static ways of being — "human being" stands out here.

***

I am here in Denmark, the vestiges of my lineage held together by tropical plants recently bought (like a palm tree cultivated in the Netherlands, which you'll learn is the world's number-one exporter of tropical plants!). And even still, there are times when I read of men like Linnaeus and find myself getting caught up in what it must have been like to have been a botanist in a time when so much was being discovered in Abya Yala, the Amazon, the Caribbean and throughout the Pacific and the African continent. But why do I put myself in the shoes of an eighteenth-century European scientist? I suppose the real question is, would an eighteenth-century Swedish scientist ever have the heart, courage and imagination to put himself in mine? I am sure I know the answer to this question.

My recent plant collection features mostly plants that are endemic to South America, the Caribbean and the Pacific Islands. I know that when I buy another Pothos, or monstera, or Caladium, I am attempting to buy a piece of my past back.

So I imagine what it was like for a man like Linnaeus to train his eyes, for the first time, on a plant like a fishbone calathea, which creeps along the jungle floor, its leaves colorful and papery. Linnaeus lived during a time when Europe met the world like the rapey Zeus, who transformed himself into a beautiful, sweet-smelling white bull in order to entice the young Phoenician princess Europa to climb upon his back. The legend goes that he dashed into the sea, abducting her, taking her to Crete, where he raped her. There's a depiction of Europa on a fourth-century find in an Eritrean woman's grave that has been named "The Mirror of Europe." Europa looks like she has an Afro if you ask me.

This was a time when economies were built on the bitterness of genocide and enslaved Black and Indigenous suffering, transformed into the sweetness of sugar for the now growing European middle class. Europeans, like all other human beings infected by civilization, have a craving for things. Cotton hardened calluses on enslaved children's hands, hands that will leave imprints on sought-after Southern bricks. Whales, birds, people, and so much more life will vanish forevermore, and here we all are: drumroll, part the curtains, please! Modernity, in all its destruction. I cannot wait until the concrete crumbles back into the earth.

Linnaeus had "apostles" whom he would often send out on voyages to bring back botanical plunder. Some would die, including plant specimens, but in a way, I imagine there is no better time to be a scientist, to truly believe that you are on par with god, that you are the one who brings order to all of this world's creation. Imagine the feeling of such power! So Zeus-like. Who has the audacity to think they can name and categorize all of creation?

Linnaeus was a pioneer in the science of identifying, naming and classifying nature, and he, in the tradition of his people, will also play a large role in scientific racism. The term "scientific racism" is an odd one. The word "scientific" gives an air of credulity where there shouldn't be any. We know that it describes the compulsion to use "science" to justify racism, something which has had devastating results, including the conception of non-Europeans as being less than human, justifying slavery and genocide. And just in case you haven't noticed, eugenics is still a thing. The Nazis didn't lose; they were absorbed. And if it weren't for them, just think, there would be no word for what Europe did to the world — the word "genocide" wasn't coined until 1948, after the Second World War.

Genocide may seem like a strong word to those who do not understand the definition of the word as outlined by the Genocide Convention adopted by the UN in 1948. Many feel that it is only applicable when used to describe the attempted complete destruction of a people, like in Armenia or Rwanda, or of German Jews in Nazi Germany. However, what about those before, when a word actually didn't exist to describe the large-scale murder of American Native, African and other Indigenous peoples throughout the world, the very foundation of European settler expansionism? There has been no justice for the descendants of enslaved Africans, Native Americans and others who were in the way of expansionism.

In the first edition of his most famous work, *Systema Naturae* (Systems of Nature), twenty-eight year-old Linnaeus, divided the living world into three kingdoms: animal, plant and mineral. Prior to Linnaeus, naturalists did not include humans in the animal kingdom as it was a widespread belief that humans were higher beings than animals; the latter were created solely for our use. Linnaeus, to his credit, actually challenged this belief by placing humans into the same group as mammals and primates.

However, the progress seems to have stopped there, as something else was at work. *Systema Naturae* would go on to be reprinted twelve times during Linnaeus's lifetime. The first nine editions (1735–56) divided the human species into four "varieties" that corresponded to the four (known) continents of the time. The "varieties" were: *Europaeus albus* (European White); *Americanus ruescene* (American reddish); *Asiaticus fuscus* (Asian tawny); and *Africanus niger* (African Black).

Over the years, he moved the order of his "varieties" around, but there was always something that remained unchanged: the Africanus variety always occupied the bottom of this hierarchy. In many editions, his descriptions of Africanus were the longest, the most detailed and physical, and also the most derogatory. Linnaeus created a racial hierarchy with Black people, associated with negative moral and physical attributes, at the very bottom.

As I pull my focus away from the specifics of Linnaeus's professional and even personal life, as I see him in light of the greater web of worlds clashing, I find myself wondering, not for the first time, about this propensity of our culture, the compulsion almost, to constantly privilege ourselves over others.

I guess this is the part that I can't seem to reconcile with Linnaeus. Part of my passion for plants comes from the undeniable intelligence that is often expressed in their very presentation. It could be in the shape of a leaf, a combination of colors, a texture that reminds you that the universe can, and often does, create masterpieces, that it has a sense of humor; and if it can create this, then what is there to say about us?

Tell me, how could you ponder the beauty of a dandelion, see its transformation from a bright yellow sun to its fluffy, intricate galactic patterning of seeds, become lost in the wonder of it, as one could imagine a man such as Linnaeus did, and still, at the end of the day, come up with something such as a racial stratification system?

We know how. There had to be justification for the violence against and exploitation of land and people. There had to be a logic in place that made Europe's colonial project a more savory affair. It is in the air that we breathe and the water that we drink. It is the very ether in which we swim. But as Deadric T. Williams noted on Twitter @doc_thoughts, "Racism is not about skin color. Racism is about having the POWER to make skin color salient for the purpose of unequally distributing resources and opportunities."

In *The Myth of Race: The Reality of Racism* by Mahmoud El-Kati, the author reminds us that "racism was not born in America. It was brought here. The idea had been initiated and well-honed among Europeans themselves, as a collection of 'races,' Nordics, Alpine, Celts, etc." For El-Kati, "race is the principle, racism is the act," and "categories of 'races' exist, but races do not."

"White supremacy," he writes, "is a modern world western European construction." But for me, the sentence that sums it all up is: "Racism is a superstition, our modern-day witchcraft."

3.

Cry for yourself
2017

But tending to plants wasn't enough to help me in life. Yes, it was uplifting discovering a pepper plant growing from my aloe (how did the seed get in there?) and to be finally be able to keep a succulent alive for longer than a year. It helps, but I needed other solutions. The situation had become tense: the year was 2017, and a man whose wealth could be traced to the federal aid his ancestors, as Europeans, were entitled to as white US arrivals, and who, in 1989, took out a full-page ad asking for the death penalty for five since-proven-innocent children, now adults, became the president of the "free" world, of the united settler states of America. On the other side of the pond, another politician, who had married a woman twenty-five years his senior he met when still a fifteen-year-old student, became the leader of the country that single-handedly (with the help of the US) face-fucked Haiti. It was the year that Hugh Hefner finally died, his body put to rest in eternal peace next to the woman whose life he almost ruined by publishing, without her permission, nude photographs of her. A man whose empire was at least partially funded by his publication of *Sugar and Spice*, which included, among other images of scantily clad children, nude pictures of a then ten-year-old Brooke Shields taken by a photographer named, aptly, Gary Gross. In the UK, the twenty-four-story Grenfell Tower went up in flames, killing seventy-two people and unleashing a scandal that revealed the contempt the government has for its poor.

I had traveled extensively in connection with my work as a writer, and although I knew that my job at the time was not a keeper, I at least knew that I still wanted to work in education. But still, I couldn't figure out how to access the joy in my life. It seemed as if the many years I had been here had been lived in a dream compounded many times by fear, anxiety, sorrow and despair. Despite the fact that I had met many people here in Copenhagen, kind people, lovely people, there was still a gaping hole in my heart — and I just couldn't figure out what was missing or why. I'm not the only one — Denmark has one of the highest rates of depression in the world. I had contemplated returning to the States many times before I did, and now, since my son would soon be approaching eighteen, this possibility was becoming more and more realistic.

But where would I return to? New York wasn't home anymore. And besides, even Copenhagen had become too much of a city for me — could I really thrive in a city as big as New York? I was tired of city living and wanted an out. I just couldn't seem to figure out how to do it.

By this point, I was suffering from a large dose of racial burnout. Although I could easily say it was from living in Scandinavia, the honest truth is that it was a culmination of many things, not least my being a foreigner in another country. The slow burn of realizing that Denmark was not necessarily the progressive, enlightened European country that its government tries to project to the rest of the world eventually scorched me. Despite a history of over two hundred years of trading in enslaved Africans, a venture that financed the development of its capital city, Copenhagen, and its harbors and industry, most Danes seemed to be confused about, if not unaware of, the source of their social democratic well-being. Denmark's involvement in the kidnapping and enslavement of Africans was not nominal — there were five forts, one of them in present-day Ghana, bearing the same name as the parliament here in Denmark: Christiansborg. All in all, Denmark is responsible for the kidnapping and enslavement of at least one hundred thousand Africans, for whom they traded Danish guns and schnaps.

And this wasn't being taught adequately in schools — which ensured that ignorance was reproduced generation after generation.

But 2017 was also the year that another type of plant would help me: Mother Aya came calling. However, I didn't travel to the Amazon rainforest. Instead, I drove about twenty minutes outside of Copenhagen on an early summer day. Yay, modernity! Although I would have preferred to travel to the Amazon rainforest for such a ceremony, I was okay with being in Copenhagen. I knew the importance of feeling comfortable where you are when you take psychedelics — and being together with others in a location I was somewhat familiar with trumped actually traveling to a foreign place.

Okay, I know some of you by this point is like, psychedelics?!? Woah there — slow down! Well, I did say that I believe in plant medicine and their power to heal. And it's not just my belief, either — it's well documented by scientific research.

I first came across ayahuasca's potential role in healing addiction, PTSD and trauma in the work of Gabor Maté, who is a global leader in the psychology of addiction and has done groundbreaking work in this field. I was introduced to his work through my good friend Kelly Curry, who has dedicated her life to health and healing. While Maté's writing mostly focuses on the link between childhood trauma and addiction, he's not afraid to remind us of how our economic, social and political systems also play a role in the demise of our mental, emotional, spiritual and physical health.

Maté has large compassionate eyes that emanate a deep love and respect for his fellow humans. He urges us to think of the body and mind as united, as well as the individual and their environment. He encourages us to seek knowledge outside of our own awareness as we tend to our fractured and traumatized selves.

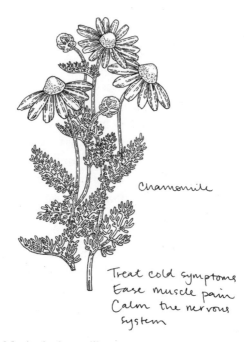

Chamomile, Matricaria chamomilla

By this time, I had found my breathing to be fast and shallow. My shoulders were all the way up to my ears, and my jaw was seemingly always clenched. Some days I had bad anxiety, and most of the time, brain fog. Slowly I began to work with my body to ease out these tensions, stretching, doing breathing exercises, taking long walks and drinking lots of chamomile for its relaxing and anti-inflammatory benefits. I learned that the opposite of toxic was tonic — something that tones, and my nervous system was in desperate need of toning. But it didn't help that my new teaching job was stressful. Between the chaos that was ensuing as a result of the school over-admitting students (and the resulting classroom shortages that sometimes meant I was without a classroom) and structural changes that came top-down from the ministry — not from people working with students — I often wondered why so many of my colleagues and I put up with the violent direction our education system was taking. It seemed that no matter what school I chose to teach in, the system was determined to infantilize its teaching staff, treating us like naughty children who needed to be kept in check. Laws were passed that made Danish and math compulsory, which had devastating consequences for students who are not academically strong. There was often very little support for the students struggling — whether mentally or academically — making it more challenging for their own intelligence to shine. The only way that many students could receive any kind of counseling through the Danish healthcare system was to agree to take anti-depressants that have been shown to trigger suicides in that exact age group. Once, at a staff meeting, I asked the other teachers why we didn't protest, at the very least out of the interest of our students. The math teacher replied, "Teachers are class traitors. Our interests are supposed to be blue collar — that's mostly our demographic — but we've been terrorized by the idea of not having a job."

Full disclosure: I try to engage with the medical system as little as possible. Even though I'm happy that we've taken so many strides in medicine and procedures, unless it's an absolute emergency, I'd rather develop the ability to attune my senses to my body and *listen*. The way I see it, no one else is ever going to be able to know my body in the way that I can. And learning about my body, in this life, has become an integral part of my healing, of my coming more into balance. And I knew it was stress that was burning me out. I was determined to do whatever I had to do to get my health back — even if it meant taking ayahuasca.

What good was it all anyway if I didn't have my health? Due to my ongoing health issues, which included constantly feeling like I was coming down with something, I approached the ayahuasca ceremony with healing as my intention. I had visited my doctor, who ran numerous tests, and aside from extremely low vitamin D and B levels (which definitely could be the reason behind my general fatigue), everything seemed fine. I did drink and smoke moderately, but other than that I was fairly healthy. I exercised, biked, lived on the fifth floor of a five-floor walk-up and have always eaten a mostly plant-based diet.

I had to find a way forward. I knew that the way my job was going and the way my body was feeling had to be tended to. I had been in Denmark for seventeen years now, and somewhere between the journey of moving to another country and becoming a parent I had found it a challenge to envision a future for myself that inspired me. There was something about my *now* that I couldn't quite put my finger on but which I found it hard to settle into; I found it hard to just *be*.

The fact of the matter is that the way I was fighting racism was not very effective or healthy. While I pride myself on my ability to disrupt, my disruptions were seemingly becoming more and more upsetting — to me the most. It was exhausting. My living in Denmark didn't help — but to be honest with you, living in any area in the West involved its own land mines of racial frustration. Did it really matter where I found myself? Was there a place where I could be at peace anywhere in this world? *In this Black and Indigenous femme body? In a world that was forged through the violent fire of land theft, enslavement and conquest?*

Was there an actual geographic space where I could feel *at home*? Safe?

I did my research. Can you imagine consuming a plant that takes you on a few hours' journey that includes healing past wounds long forgotten, or, as many others' testimonies seem to indicate, even physical ailments? What about a plant that seems to help some people deal with PTSD? Addiction? Depression? And add racism in there, because that was a large reason I was seeking the medicine.

There's ample evidence from various scholarly reports that this brew, ayahuasca, can assist our species in reconnecting with ourselves, each other and the natural world around us. What better medicine could this world use as we sit on the brink of climate disaster?

I know that there are reports of over-harvesting of the plants that compose this brew. But I also know that there are sustainable ways to obtain it, and I know that this ceremony has been co-opted and abused many times, especially by the West. Do your research. I am not telling you to go take ayahuasca.

Ayahuasca
Banisteriopsis caapi
Madre Ayahuasca
Sacred medicine
Vine of the Soul

Ayahuasca vine, Banisteriopsis caapi

Originally from South America, the concoction is usually composed of the ayahuasca vine (*Banisteriopsis caapi*), the chacruna leaf (*Psychotria viridis*), the chagropanga vine, and an assortment of other plants. "Ayahuasca" can refer either the vine itself or the brew — of which the vine is one of the constituents. It takes hours to prepare, as it is the chemical composition of the two plants that provides the user with the psychedelic experience. The hallucinogenic substance that the ayahuasca vine contains, dimethyltryptamine (DMT), is one we also secrete from our brains. But if we were to just eat it, our stomach enzyme monoamine oxidase would block its effects. So, somehow, a long time ago, folks learned how to combine these plants so that their psychedelic properties are allowed to take effect.

Its effect induces hallucinations that include, but are not limited to, visitations from other beings, feelings of spiritual ecstasy, deep connection and even enlightenment. There's the other side as well — I know folks who have plummeted into the bowels of hell while on this stuff. It's not for the faint of heart. The experience can be intense.

The ayahuasca vine — which looks very much like its Latin name, a rope banister of sorts — along with its cohorts in herbal healing, is said to have been in use for millennia for various aspects of healing. This idea, however, has received a little pushback, with some suggesting that ayahuasca use may not be a ritual spanning back millennia but a new one, picked up by the people in a demonstration of how culture changes, updates and accommodates.

Western science still cannot understand how this chemical concoction was figured out by the otherwise "primitive" folk of the Amazon, and continues to be baffled by Amazonians' vast botanical knowledge, all of which they claim came to them from the plants themselves. To let you know just how real this is, the chemical compound that we use for anesthesia today was borrowed from them (with no financial compensation, of course). Their *curare* — an admixture of various plants in which they then dipped their darts — would paralyze their prey when hit. There are many different concoctions of this — each providing a specific type of paralysis that the hunter may wish for their prey. This would later revolutionize medical anesthesia.

So, when the opportunity presented itself to take ayahuasca, I jumped at it. Ida, my Danish friend who I had met in the Nineties in New York at Flux, was scheduled to attend a retreat. Knowing Ida before I moved to Denmark greatly facilitated my landing there. She and her family opened their hearts and home to me in a way that challenges Scandinavia's global reputation of being a closed culture.

"I'm in!" I let her know. We were in her small garden in her Copenhagen home, sharing a pot of peppermint tea. We sat under a fig tree as we enjoyed an early spring day.

"Let's do it!" she confirmed, as a smile danced on her lips and we toasted our colorful tea cups.

It was on a sunny Friday afternoon when I ran down the stairs of my Østerbro apartment building, hugging my pillow to my chest to Ida's parked car outside. We were instructed to bring a sleeping bag, pillow and a sketch pad with some coloring pens, among other things. I hopped in her waiting car, and together with our mutual friend Rikke, we drove the twenty minutes or so out of Copenhagen.

None of us knew what to expect, but we all knew that we were looking for: some kind of healing. We had all been on the *dieta* — the simple diet that's recommended for at least three days before taking aya: No meat. No sugar. No marijuana. No coffee. No cigarettes. No sex.

In the car, we spoke about why we decided to embark on this journey:

"I just want to get out of this depression!" Rikke said, her long, dirty-blonde hair curly and cascading over her shoulders. Throughout the years, I had learned from Rikke about her ongoing bout with depression. Rikke doesn't conform to the stifling codes of the heteronormative, and we'd often joke about the spaces her various identities often demanded as a Danish, Jewish lesbian. Together, we've created a YouTube show for her in our head called "'I don't eat gluten' — the adventures of a neurotic in Copenhagen."

"I feel like I'm being called to aya," Ida chimed in, echoing something that you will hear again and again from many who decide to try aya, including myself. Many describe their participating in an aya ceremony as a calling, believing that the plant itself has invited them, whether through their interest or even in dreams.

We drove to the tiny town, about half an hour out of the city, where we were scheduled to have our ceremony. Nothing in Copenhagen is ever too far away. The town, with its green landscape and close proximity to the ocean, was a welcome destination. We pulled up to a camping site and saw a small group waiting, sitting around, and despite the dieta I mentioned before, smoking, chatting and drinking coffee. It was a gorgeous Danish day; the sun was shining, and the vibe felt good.

There was enough time before the start of the ceremony for us to talk among ourselves. I was relieved to find the atmosphere relaxed and open. I was pleased to chat and hear about why they had decided, like me, to gather that Friday evening at a camping ground to drink this medicine from the Amazon. What struck me the most was that everyone I spoke to had not only shown up for some personal healing but understood that there was a collective nature to this ceremony as well. From the beginning it was clear that it was also about being there for each other.

The facilitators included a man from Spain who referred to himself as a *shaman* — as well as some others there to support him. Usually, I get leery when I hear Westerners refer to themselves as such, if only due to the general blind spots and insensitivity that seem to be inherent in our belief systems. But I was desperate, which made me open.

There were a couple of musicians — a guitarist and someone with a handpan. At that point, I still had no idea what to expect. I had no idea what I was getting into. I only knew that I was going to drink something that could possibly offer me some kind of healing. From the other twenty-something participants, I learned some of the various reasons that brought them there:

A tattooed woman with short red hair wanted answers as to what she should do with her life. She worked in a circus and had been itching to move on, but had no idea of where to go. Her voice was a mixture of adventure and too many cigarettes.

Another, a tall, thin hairdresser, with his hair in a bun, wanted relief from his addictions.

And yet another was conflicted about the relationship they were in.

There were physical ailments, depression, anxiety and wishes for relief from this very thing that we found ourselves swimming in — life.

It's early summer, and although it's late, the evening sun can still be seen outside. It's Denmark, so this time of the year we almost have midnight sun. I can hear the sound of others keeling over and retching into their buckets, which were each paired with a mattress on the floor. The *icaros*, which Monica Gagliano — author of *Thus Spoke the Plant: A Remarkable Journey of Groundbreaking Scientific Discoveries and Personal Encounters with Plants*, among other titles — describes as medicine songs that are used to deliver the medicine to us, fill the air as though the music itself, being played by a guitarist, a drummer and a singer, was a butterfly, fluttering throughout the room and into our senses.

I was crying as I had never cried before. I was lying on a single flat mattress in a large room along with twenty-six other people who are retching, moaning and groaning. It was as if I was in the midst of a disaster site — everyone was disabled by a great level of discomfort. The tears seemed to pour from deep within my hardened heart and out through my eyes, nonstop. Copious amounts of mucus flowed from my nose. I blew profusely yet uselessly into the disintegrating tissue. The dissolving tissue was evidence of how much I had been crying. And just when I thought I was about to stop, my mind became flooded again with thoughts of the earth and what we, humans, were doing to her.

I had been gifted with the ability to feel the earth as a being, like myself. I could see — no, better than that, I could *feel* — the interconnectedness of it all: the giant web of life rendering not one being too small, too insignificant. All of us in that room were connected to each other — I saw it, the light of connection that emanates from us all to each and everything, even the dirt. I laughed when I thought about the fact that if there were indeed a hierarchy in life, then dirt would be on top. Kaipo Kekona, a farmer on the island of Maui, said it best in a *Guardian* article: "We believe that the land is the chief, the people its servants."

It wasn't long between the time I drank the bitter, thick concoction and when the tears started to flow. Everyone had drunk from the cup after openly declaring to each other what our respective intentions for the evening were, and as I sat there on my mattress, hearing all those around me retch in what seemed so much like misery, I straightened my back, closed my eyes and was thankful that the vomiting had not seemed to hit me. I could feel myself drawing up my spine, straightening my back as I sat in the lotus position, and felt myself the queen I knew myself to be. Until I, too, reached for my bucket and began to barf unroyally into it.

Flashing through my mind were scenes of large dozers, mining trucks, driving over large expanses of pitted land, digging and drilling far down into the earth, whether to extract raw materials such as gold and copper and precious stones, to frack or extract fossil fuel or to bury pipelines. Our actions toward the earth seemed violent from this new perspective I was now gifted with, which in turn would cause me again to double over in grief and break into uncontrollable sobs. It was as if I had a fault line of grief running through my body, threatening to break me in two.

Since my ayahuasca trip, I have looked into mining and found that, as I had suspected, it is violent. Mining issues include water misuse, pollution — of surface and groundwater as well as soil pollution — loss of biodiversity, erosion, sinkholes, labor abuses and of course the health of the population close by. Because of the extent of our consumerism and lack of substantial recycling programs, mining activity has, in fact, only gone up. Many of our raw materials are sourced from the Global South, and quite often, we're not truly paying the price — they are.

Suddenly, I felt a dryness in my mouth. I reached for my water bottle and drank as if I had never drank before. The water tasted perfect — sweet. It was clear and clean. As I drank, I could feel the water flow through my body; every single cell refreshed. *Mní wichòni*: the Lakota saying, water is life. *I must take care of the water*, I thought as I gulped as much water as I possibly could.

It had only been a few months before that the Indigenous-led movement that became known as #NODAPL began. Water protectors went to Standing Rock to protest the construction of the Dakota Access Pipeline, a 1,172-mile-long oil pipeline that, when completed, would carry oil through four states, beneath two major rivers and sacred burial grounds.

My attention was fully trained on our planet, our home, the one on which I found myself existing yet knew so little about: earth. I thought about how ironic the urgency to explore outer space seemed when our own planet remained so mysterious it might as well have been Mars. Mars has always been our culture's ultimate symbol of alienation; and alienated we were — not from some planet out in space, but here, from our own sacred relationship with the earth. Mars is also the planet of war — and where else in this universe, *as far as we know*, is there as much war as we earthlings seem to engage in? And lastly, Mars is masculine energy — the energy of the patriarchal power that has come to bring our planet out of balance. This is not about gender — but energy. Sometimes I wonder if the universe appears to us as it does because of our own projections.

It also became clear to me that the elements, if we listen, are the conduits of much information. The winds, the rains, even the fly that's buzzing annoyingly over your food: earth was constantly communicating with us if only we listened. But that was it, wasn't it? I finally was able to see — the modernity project was premised upon jamming up our connection to this force, keeping us in survival mode, in a mentality of scarcity and fear. I was able to see how this alienation from the nurturing power of the earth seemed to be a global operating system, one designed to keep us trapped thinking we were separate, special, apart from other aspects of nature and in a kind of technological enslavement.

I felt the pain she (earth) must surely feel when we dig up mines for extraction, when we mindlessly pour poison into her from the innumerable factories and industrial plants dotting the planet and through the industrial farming that is promoted in our world but which seems to produce even more waste while, still, people are starving, despite the fact that we have more than enough to feed the world five times over. I thought about the oil spills, the weed killer and all of the plastic that is choking our seas. I wept for all of the destruction we were doing to all of our other relations, the animals, the insects, the earth herself. A wave of nausea lurched from my stomach. I grabbed the bucket at the side of my mattress and proceeded to retch violently into it. Although my eyes were closed, I saw the vomit leave my body and vortex its way into the bucket. The vomit spiraled into a series of cartoon-like tiles. Each small tile bore the skull-and-bones emblem — the symbol of poison.

As I seemed to heave out the entire contents of my being into my constant and reliable partner, the black plastic bucket, I felt as if I was the earth herself, and through my purging, she too was being purged. Each time I doubled over to vomit into the bucket, I felt that I was giving the earth some release, some cleansing. I could feel that this was what was happening to my body, as well — a cleanse, a release. What was all this poison I was holding onto in my body?

I felt such a connection to the earth, and it made so much sense. I grieved when I thought of how disconnected my life seemed from her. I cried, bawled and shook my head in shame as I thought about all the horrible things we did to our mother. The thoughts about earth came flooding in, and with them the tears. All I can remember is blowing my nose continuously as what seemed like buckets and buckets of mucus flowed out of my nose. And then I heard a voice: *Don't cry for me. Cry for yourself.*

I know that for a lot of folks the idea of being in a room full of others puking sounds highly disgusting. And for a good reason. Well, if that wasn't bad enough — folks were shitting too.

While I, too, admit that it does sound disgusting as hell, there was also something quite soothing about it. The vomiting and the shitting peeled away whatever façade we had all walked in there with. The shitting, the vomiting, the crying — all of it — were universally humbling. It was a place where we all needed to be. It made the situation a lot more human.

Every so often, I was able to tune back into the room and see those around me. The various experiences seemed to be running the gamut between episodes of extreme joy, ecstasy even, and immense sorrow, grief and fear. Later, after the ceremony, when we have all shared our experiences, I will learn that for many there, memories of early childhood sexual abuse came up. Every emotion possible seemed to be in that room. One participant who was next to me appeared to me as though an angel, floating in the air as she danced to the soft music being played. I looked over at Ida to check in. She was lying down on the mattress next to me, wearing a pink satin eye mask. She communicated to me that it was challenging, but she was coping. We both checked in on Rikke, who seemed to be struggling even more.

My ayahuasca journey, like so many others, was intense. It was so intense that I took much less the following evening, and I'm really on the fence about whether I would ever take her again. In a way, I don't believe I have to. She ran down everything that I needed to reconcile with — including unearthing feelings I had long ago buried deep within my heart, such as about friends who have passed, relationships that ended. And in some way, it was as if the tears that I cried were all that sorrow and hurt that had calcified my heart, which was now melting, revealing a softer, more vulnerable and open one.

When I finally stopped crying, my head felt much lighter. I had emptied my head of what seemed to be buckets of mucus. As I lay on my mattress, the soft sounds of the guitar and *icaros* could still be heard — the most beautiful of songs. Although I could not understand the language, there was something calming about it. I slowly started to feel as though I was on a boat — the retching and misery all around me seemed to awaken a memory, the soft words in Spanish another layer that transported me to another time and place.

With closed eyes, I felt I was on a journey on a wooden ship across the Atlantic. This ship was taking its human cargo from the shores of Africa to the Caribbean. With the whispers in Spanish, I heard the crew of the ship. I did not feel terror, however. Rather, I felt I was being shown something. From this space that I had entered, I was able to see and, to some extent, even feel — without any fear whatsoever — that perilous journey that many of my ancestors were forced to embark on.

Lineage, I believe, can be a map to our humanity. Learning and understanding the historical context of the stories of our ancestors is vital to our understanding of ourselves and even each other. Every human lineage on this planet includes stories of suffering, terror, love, joy and compassion, among other emotions. It is what makes us human. I also know that in the region now known as Europe, the enslavement of others has been happening for thousands of years. And although I also have to reconcile with the very uncomfortable idea that there were a few Africans who participated in and benefited from the trade, I know that there were many Africans who refused to participate in the kidnapping, torture, and enslavement of other Africans; that there were people, and kingdoms even, that made enslavement illegal and went on liberating expeditions to release the captured. We have always resisted. I also know that the process of racializing enslavement is a uniquely European one.

But still, as a descendant of enslaved Africans, I can attest to the fact that there has never been any real attempt to address our unique needs as a people who have experienced enslavement and displacement, to say the least. On another level, I also understand the connections between the enslavement of my ancestors and state-sanctioned murder (when the police murder us), mass incarceration (when the state confines us), poverty, criminalization, addiction and trauma. Every country that benefited from the enslavement of Africans has a responsibility to rectify the conditions in which too many of us, their descendants, are forced to live. Their number-one priority should be implementing programs of restorative justice for this global community, of which I am a part. That is what justice looks like.

Back in the ayahuasca room, as I heard the others groan and vomit around me, it was as if they, too, the occupants of this room, were also on this boat; their vomiting, the general malaise that everyone in that room was experiencing were as if they, too, were going through the horrors of what had been done in their nation's name. In my hallucinogenic daze, the room became a holding space for the collective misery of it all. It was as if their misery directly corresponded to their remorse. *If only such a thing could happen in real life*, I remember thinking. I was reminded that this, too, was a possible road to take on the subject of racial healing. That's not to say I've ever seen such remorse in real life. There has never been any true remorse, no real effort at amending what Europe has done to the rest of the world, including my ancestors. Denmark, like all other European countries, has never done this. The fact that they don't teach their children about Denmark's deliberate dehumanization of Black people and others in order to build its own wealth has deep ramifications for the continuation and reproduction of the shitshow that began in 1492.

I had come into this ayahuasca journey with a bevy of racially traumatic experiences behind me — including health issues that were very much related to these experiences. The truth is, ayahuasca helped me feel deeply, something that is sometimes immensely difficult for me to do. I had been walking around with a wall around me as protection, which only seemed to be exacerbated by the snowballing of microaggressions one is subjected to in the West. I was hoping that I would be better prepared for the next bout of shit spouting out of someone's mouth or for the next time someone showed up to a party in blackface. I felt like I always had to be on guard. The triggers felt physical, and at the time I didn't fully make the connection between the visceral power that is embedded in race and racism. I had not yet come across Resmaa Menakem, whose work focuses on the effects of trauma on the human body and its particular effects on our nervous system especially in how it relates to race. I didn't understand the role of our vagus nerve and how it is connected to trauma, or how you can work on it, tone it, and so become stronger and less excitable. I didn't understand the visceral effects of that holy grail of the West — free speech. "Sticks and stones may break my bones, but words will never hurt me," we were taught as children.

However, Lisa Feldman Barrett, PhD, has uncovered that words do hurt us physically. As explained in an article on

Ideas. Ted.com entitled, "People's words and actions can actually shape your brain." Barrett sheds a lot of light onto why so many of us feel physically triggered when we hear racist words or see racist imagery.

New experiences change the wiring of our brains, she tells us, due to a neural feature called "plasticity." This process happens gradually every day. "Little by little, your brain becomes tuned and pruned as you interact with others." It's not just words that effect other people, even raising your voice or even an eyebrow can affect what goes on in others' bodies, such as the chemicals released into their bloodstream and their heart rate. This is why, she explains, holding someone's hand during a moment of distress can have such a calming effect.

But it's not just our actions that regulate each other; we can also do this with words. "A kind word may calm you, like when a friend gives you a compliment at the end of a hard day. And a hateful word may cause your brain to predict a threat and flood your bloodstream with hormones, squandering precious resources from your body budget." Barrett explains that our "body budget" is the sum of the ways our brains manage the bodily resources that we use every day. If we are under stress, our body budget tends to get eaten up needlessly by feelings of fear and distress, taxing our systems furthermore. I guess, by this time, my body budget was in the red.

The power of words can cross great distances — think about a text from a loved one who lives in a foreign country — and even through time — think of the ways in which ancient scriptures can offer so much comfort today. "Research shows that we all can tweak one another's nervous systems with mere words in very physical ways."

This is groundbreaking when you think about the idea of freedom of speech, and when we live in cultures where hate speech continues to be protected — especially when those cultures encourage and execute violence toward the global majority. Feldman Barrett continues: "Words, then, are tools for regulating human bodies. Other people's words have a direct effect on your brain activity and your bodily systems, and your words have the same effect on other people. Whether you intend that effect is irrelevant. It's how we're wired."

She goes on to explain how stress can impact our brain and even cause illness. The various stresses include "physical abuse, verbal aggression, social rejection, neglect, and the countless other creative ways that we social animals torment one another".

Our nervous systems, she explains, are bound up with "the behavior of other humans, for better or for worse." What's the solution to this? "A realistic approach to our dilemma is to realize that freedom always comes with responsibility. We are free to speak and act, but we are not free from the consequences of what we say and do. We might not care about those consequences, or we might not agree that these consequences are justified, but they nonetheless have costs that we all pay.

***

I thought about my son and his birth and about how — despite the fact that I gave birth in a Northern European hospital, among the best in the world — I had almost died. When I arrived at the birthing center, I could tell something was wrong. It didn't help that my mother had traveled all the way from the States to be with me during this important time and that, at the last minute, she turned to me and said, "I'm not going with you into the delivery room. I don't want to see you like that. I'm scared." I remember thinking, *What the fuck is going to happen in that delivery room that she knows about* (she's given birth to three children) *that I obviously don't know?*

Now, when I look at my mother, I am able to see how her own traumas have frozen her — even physically, as expressed in the way she stands, sits and fidgets. My mother always seems as if she wants to shrink away, never fully presenting herself in social spaces. I hadn't yet realized the extent to which my mother's past trauma impacted our relationship, as I have been too busy investing in overcoming my own.

I was in labor for over twenty-four hours, and throughout the entire time, I asked for a caesarean. "Everyone says that," they assured me, laughing even. Finally, at the last minute, a pink-faced man wearing a white surgical gown came storming into the delivery room. He shoved everyone to the side and held what looked like a toilet plunger. He proceeded to suction my baby out of my body — my baby had been inside of me too long and was now in danger. Because I was denied access to prenatal care by the Danish government for the first three months of my pregnancy, we were unable to monitor my pregnancy sufficiently. Laws were recently passed to make it more difficult for foreign spouses of Danes to immediately access the socialized healthcare system. When you think about the link between prenatal care and infant mortality, you have to wonder why the Danish government would institute such a policy that directly impacts the health of both mother and child. You begin to realize why there is such a high instance of infant mortality among the Somali community, for example.

The situation was tense: both my life and my baby were in danger.

As I lay there on the bed, my legs up and far apart, and as he stood there between my legs, pulling so hard that he actually put his foot up on the table, I remember thinking I had never felt so dehumanized in my entire life. When my child was forcibly pulled out of me, he was placed in his father's arms, and they both were unceremoniously kicked out of the delivery room. My placenta hadn't come out, and I was in the process of losing what would amount to two liters of blood. My life was on the line.

This birthing experience impacted us as a family in ways that I think we're only now starting to understand. I'm sure it was a part of my postpartum depression, and it has definitely ensured that motherhood is a country I'm not in a rush to visit again. I would later learn that in Denmark, students of medicine are taught about the cultural differences that exist in terms of how people express themselves. Some cultures are louder than others, they are told, while others can tolerate more pain. I wonder how the medical staff saw me on that day and how much communication, even with my own mother, had impacted my ability to give birth.

During my ayahuasca journey, I also had intermittent visions in which I saw myself and everyone else in the room as part of the same gigantic leaf. It was as if we were each nestled in a plant cell like it was some sort of pod. I felt safe, loved. My head and heart were so much lighter.

The next day, when I woke up, I knew I had done the right thing. I knew that I had taken medicine that had corrected me physically, emotionally, spiritually and mentally. It was a powerful brew, and I knew it would be years before I ever did it again, if I ever chose to do so. I knew that there were many lessons to unpack from my evening with her. I could go on and on about what happened to me that night — but I think it's important to be careful about what we share about these rituals, as some messages were clearly for me alone.

According to modern science, believing that hallucinations are real is the very definition of psychosis. The hallucinations I experienced that day, of vomiting up all the toxins that were poisoning the earth, of being on a slave ship full of miserable Danes retching over their own ancestors' involvement in trafficking my ancestors, of having three jaguars walk into the room, surround me and tell me, telepathically, that they are my protectors, of the toilet's ability to accept my gratitude as it sits there and receives my shit — well, they didn't need to be real. They felt real enough to endow me with the emotional information I needed to work with toward my own personal healing. That evening I felt what Monica Gagliano has proven — that plants are intelligent and capable of communication.

All of that crying and sniffling cleared my head in a way that I hadn't felt in years. I had had a build-up of mucus — which as a lifetime smoker makes a lot of sense. Who knew I had been holding all this mucus in my body? By the time I had stopped crying, my hearing had become clearer and my chest and head lighter. I knew this was part of the physical healing I had approached the ritual of ayahuasca for.

***

Ayahuasca is definitely not for everyone. Everybody's healing journey is different, and as many other folks who have partaken in the ceremony believe, like my friend Ida, Mother Aya is a calling. I'm sharing with you how my intuition led me to a group of powerful plants that have been instrumental in shifting my focus. I actually came out of the experience feeling healed of my fury, a fury that was destroying me. But the ceremony is one thing. How do I integrate all of this new information into my life?

There's a lot of controversy surrounding its use — and I'm not here to argue about that. As I've mentioned before, my interest in ayahuasca emerged upon finding out about its use in dealing with addiction and post-traumatic stress disorder. And to be honest, I was desperate. I came out of my ayahuasca experience with something powerful and valuable. I came out with the realization that another existence is possible.

And till this day, even years after participating in the ceremony, in which I have never participated again, I still hear her voice, gently reprimanding me, "Don't cry for me, Lesley. Cry for yourself. I'll be okay. But what about you?"

4.

Don't quit your day job
January 2019

Yeah, Mother Aya, you're right! What about *me*? Who am I to *pity* the earth? I had my own problems.

By 2018, I had finally had enough, and quit my job. After much deliberation, I decided to leave Denmark. I left a teaching job in Copenhagen that, although I loved it, made me feel as though I was doing more harm than good. Take, for example, the plight of having no classroom. I was expected, among other things, to keep a class together that was shuffled around. One day I had to instruct them in the hallway, another in a classroom that was already occupied. It all became too much, however, when Mehdi stopped coming to school.

Mehdi was the same age as my own child — he was twenty at the time he landed in my classroom, but looked even younger. Mehdi was one of the few students who would give me shit about being American, and I took it. He wasn't mean about it, but he was correct in any connections he made between the country of my origin and his. He was never mean — but did come off as extremely broken. He had left Afghanistan with his family when he was sixteen and had gotten separated from them in Turkey. He had not seen them since.

There is a mental health epidemic happening in our world. In 2019, before the pandemic, fifty million people in the united settler states suffered from mental health issues. This mental health crisis is not about chemicals (or the lack thereof) in our brain, as has been promoted in the past. In Denmark, if you are in need of support, you *have to go on medication.* The issue with this is that the medication can sometimes be dangerous. It can take away your ability to feel, encourage you to self-harm and even push some toward suicide. Medication is not the only way of dealing with depression. If it works for you, great. But it's not for everyone. This is why I personally sought other treatments outside of the system. I know, for example, that micro-dosing with psilocybin can spur your neurons to re-establish connections lost due to depression. Yale research found that psilocybin can "increase the density of dendritic spines, small protrusions found on nerve cells which aid in the transmission of information between neurons," as well as echoing the research of the previously mentioned Lisa Feldman Barrett, PhD, that "Chronic stress and depression are known to reduce the number of these neuronal connections."

I remember the day I learned that the US government had decided to bomb Afghanistan in response to 9/11. I remember looking over at my own child, barely one. I was lying on the bed and he was playing — we were both in his room and I remember the day as though it was yesterday. I thought of all the families, all the mothers and fathers, who now had to face the specter of US bombs falling from the sky. I shuddered. Now, years later, I saw the "collateral damage" of my government's foreign policy. I had also noticed that on Mehdi's arms were all the markings of someone who was harming themselves. It was just one of those frustrating situations that many of us as teachers often find ourselves in: facing another human being who is clearly suffering and in pain but being unable to fully address this being's condition.

My colleagues were mostly amazing — incredibly dedicated and doing their best given the situation. But there was something about moving around students, creating an unnecessary chaos for students, many of whom were fleeing war, that didn't sit right with me.

And despite a fantastical ayahuasca journey, or perhaps because of it, I felt like I wanted to begin exploring a different lifestyle, one that was more in line with who I am — not one in which I found myself doing things that I was so obviously against, like continuing at the school. I also wanted to figure out where in this world I fit. I had been in Denmark for over twenty years — was I meant to stay? Return to the States? Or…?

I had a newly published book, and like in all other situations of restlessness, I bought a plane ticket. I embarked on a seven-city US tour, including traveling to Trondheim, Norway, Helsinki, Finland, and Paris, France. My son was officially an adult now, and we had both agreed that wherever I decided to be would be a win for him as well, if only by creating more of the distance and space needed for exercises of reflection and having different experiences.

I had only been in New York for a few weeks when my mother called to let me know that my grandmother had been admitted to the hospice. "I think this is it," my mother said, her voice both heavy and childlike. Theirs was a special relationship — my grandmother and my mother, her first child. Mummy Hildred, my grandmother, would often tell us how little she knew about anything when she was pregnant with my mother — that when the doctor said to her that my mother was breeching, she was too embarrassed to ask the doctor what that meant. "Beryl was born backwards!" my grandmother would joke in response to my mother. "Her ass came out first! That's why she's like that!" My grandmother spoiled my mother. Throughout their lives, my mother always remained my grandmother's little girl. Looking back, I understand better how the fact that both my grandparents were orphaned had impacted their own parenting, and their relationship to their children, my mother included.

When I arrived at my grandmother's room, I could hear Sinatra belting out *New York, New York*. I smiled, as my grandmother had always liked him. Her breathing was laborious, like a fish out of water. I held her hand, and the gentle smell of bay leaf met me. I placed my head on her chest, listened to her heart beating slowly and rhythmically, held her hand and thought how each breath of hers was a step closer to death. I could see downtown Brooklyn right outside her window, a place I had frequented as a child, getting sweatshirts with zodiac patterns, brass belt buckles that spelled your name, gold teeth even. Unfortunately, the downtown Brooklyn skyline, full of skyscrapers and cranes, changing throughout the years, obstructed the sky. Just then, Rick Astley's "Never Gonna Give You Up" came on, and I laughed. "You used to love this one, Hildred. Rick was your boy!" And I laughed, as visions of my grandmother snapping her fingers and dancing to Rick Astley were a very beautiful gift.

Suddenly, she gasped. And then her breath returned, punctuating the air. There was a rhythm, albeit winding down, like the ending of a song.

"Hildred," my younger cousin would ask her when we were children, "why you so dread?" And all of us grandkids would laugh; her laugh, however, was louder than ours. But, while my grandmother was a lively woman, one full of zest, there were of course other sides to her as well. Sometimes, as a child, I would see how my grandmother's face would twist with worry. Sometimes the worries had to do with the concerns she had for her children, other times they were financial. Sometimes, I think, my grandmother suffered from great bouts of shame.

For my grandmother, shame reared its head in a multitude of ways. Often, she'd express shame that she had left her youngest son, attributing his relaxed attitude toward academics to this. She would try to alleviate this by materially indulging him. Sometimes, she would express shame about my grandfather's drinking. When she would collapse under stress and worry, I learned that sometimes my grandmother's faith waivered.

Sometimes she'd express frustration that none of her children had fancy degrees or jobs. "Look at so-and-so, son," she'd lament to her youngest son, Vince, when they fought, "he just became an engineer."

Vince would suck his teeth in response. "You think that's the kind of thing Jesus would notice?" He wasn't being rude. He meant it. He was a dreamy child, sensitive. As a teenager, he loved playing football and listening to Black Sabbath. It wasn't that he wasn't intelligent; it was just that school didn't do anything for him.

Once, when I lived with her in Trinidad, she experienced a severe breakdown. The family called it a stroke, but all I could see were bottles of medication, rosary beads and neighbors visiting to pray over her. It was the only time I had ever seen my grandmother incapacitated, and fear gripped me: Who would care for me if my grandmother was gone? Although only an adolescent, I was keenly aware that I had no one else.

My grandmother spoke in the language of miracles and faith — something I witnessed that was sometimes difficult for her to reconcile. My grandmother wanted a family who had performed well in school and professionally. I know she wanted doting children who chauffeured her to and from church. Yet, I know she still loved us despite our inability to deliver on all these things.

Now, in the hospice room, my grandmother's face registered very little but peace. I stood by her side and studied the woman whose body I knew so well — her ridged nails, strong legs and large stomach that she would often bound in a girdle. I placed my head next to hers, aware that her smell, mingled with Vicks VapoRub, would be no more. As a child, I loved how she smelled of dinner mints, Canadian healing oil, soft candle, Limacol and bay rum.

And even on her deathbed, my grandmother was beautiful. First I marveled at the smoothness of her radiant skin. Then I chuckled, "You look sexy, Mummy Hildred."

"Sexy?" she'd say. "Me don't want anything to do with that!" And we'd both laugh.

"But seriously though," I whisper into her ear. "Hildred, you look stunning." I smiled; in a family that has always valued beauty, that was indeed one of the best things I could have said to her.

I sat on a fold-out couch in her hospice room and took out my knitting. I began knitting from the red-and-cream yarn ball of soft wool, my needles bamboo. The knitting was rhythmic, and it lulled me into a blissful meditative state as my grandmother's breathing became deeper and deeper and further apart. Sometimes, I'd interrupt my knitting to stand or sit by her side. I held her hand and stroked her silky gray hair. I hugged her and told her how much I loved her.

At some points throughout the night, I'd hear Sinatra's voice: "Start spreading the news…", the CD player giving my grandmother her last bevy of her favorite music: parang, steel-pan renditions of David Rudder's "Trini to De Bone"…

"Did I tell you that I published my first book?" I asked her as I picked up a stitch in my knitting. "I put all the family business out there." I eyed her as if she knew what I was saying. "You would have hated it." I chuckled.

"You could go now, Mummy," I whispered. "It's okay to let go.

***

They say your hearing is the last sense to leave you when you die. If that is the case, then I guess it makes complete sense that the last thing my grandmother heard was my mother and I arguing. Over a fur coat. Let me explain.

My mother was now retired, but her last job was as caretaker to an octogenarian, Shelley Wu. Shelley came from an affluent Shanghai family but was the self-described black sheep, and Shelly loved to gamble. This is why I suspected he loved my mother, as she would accompany him to Atlantic City against the doctor's order. I could see them: him with his walker, my mother in shimmering clothes, seated next to him at a blackjack table.

"Shelley gave me his mother's mink coat. Do you want it?" she asked me one day. Did I want the mink coat of a deceased matriarch? There was something about the idea that I loved. It isn't that I'm into fur — I wouldn't wear it outside. But it was vintage and had a story. I'd wear it inside, while I wrote. Once, I tried on a friend's grandmother's fur that she had inherited and enjoyed the feel of it against my skin, how safe I felt inside of it. I saw myself in a cottage somewhere in the Danish countryside — it's cold outside, I have the wood burning in the oven, and there I am, wearing my fur coat as I write. I became excited by the idea.

My mother had agreed to bring the coat to me at the hospital the next day. I was excited about the legacy of it, the style of it, the romance and the distraction it provided from the fact that my grandmother was finally leaving us. But when my mother showed up the following day, I met an agitated woman.

"I can't find the coat." Her face was worried. "I could only find my fake one."

"I think I gave her the real one instead," she continued, hanging her head down. We were both standing on either side of her mother, whose breathing was even slower and more pronounced than the day before. My mother explained that she had given her fake fur away to someone, but now she realized she had given them the real one.

"You gave away your mink coat?!" I asked in disbelief.

And that's when I noticed.

"Mom."

"Yes, Lesley?"

"Mummy, Mummy stopped breathing." I always called my grandmother Mummy because I felt she was my mother. Then my mother's face collapsed, and her body became deflated.

"I'm scared," my mother said, her voice low.

"Don't be scared," I told her. "It will be okay. Go get the nurse."

I suppose it made sense that the last thing my grandmother heard was my mother and me arguing.

My mother left the room to alert the nurses on duty. I was left alone with my grandmother's body, which, no longer animated by breath, now seemed as empty as an abandoned house. My mother returned with the nurse, a friendly Filipino man who understood the importance of losing a matriarch.

"They'll be coming to take her body away," the nurse said, a gentle hand on my shoulder. I was still at her side, not able to move. I didn't want to move. I wasn't sure I would be able to cope with leaving her.

"Can I stay with her until they come?"

"Yes," he said.

I waited in the room until two tall men came in with the body bag. One had sandy-colored hair, the other dark. I still couldn't bring myself to leave. What will happen to me without my grandmother? "Can I stay here until you take her out?" The two men were dressed in blue scrubs. I sat there and watched them prepare her body — they bound her arms and legs.

"We're going to put her in the bag now. Are you sure you want to stay?"

I nodded yes.

They lifted her limp body into the black bag, zipped it up and placed her on the stretcher.

"You're going to have to leave now," the brown-faced man said.

Part Two

1.

Rematriation
March 2019

My grandmother — the woman who once scrubbed, blued and starched my white Providence School shirt and left it on the line to dry — was gone. My grandmother — the woman who woke up every morning with the rising sun to roast bake on the cast iron *tawa*. The warm bake melts my butter over the *zabaca*, which I sprinkle generously with Grandaddy's homemade pepper sauce. My grandmother — who migrated from Trinidad in the late Sixties to the promise of economic mobility in the US, leaving her three-year-old son to do so — had been diagnosed with Alzheimer's in 2007, and now, in 2019, she had finally let go of this plane. Alzheimer's, like some Spanish conqueror, had subdued her once-sovereign mind. Gone were her Hail Marys, feisty cuss-outs and the sucking of the teeth that came from the ships of the enslaved. It had been many years of not hearing her sing slightly off-key, "Audrey, where you get that sugah from?"

Come home, her death whispers to me.

Her eternal rest was a love letter to me, a love letter to go home.

But what is *home* to a woman like me? Is it the apartment in Brooklyn I lived in many, many years before, a home no longer there — with my father's Hammond in the living room, my mother applying her make-up, dressed in a polyester slip, in front of the bathroom mirror; my sister reading *Narrative of the life of Frederick Douglass, an American Slave* under her giant Jimi Hendrix poster over her bed; my brother at the foot of his bed, turning the pedals of an upside-down bike as he tests the oily chain? No, it can't be there — that home is too far in the past, a childhood long gone, all three children fated to leave by the time we turned sixteen.

Or is it the home I once shared with my grandmother and my mother's youngest sister? We were three generations living in a small Brooklyn apartment. I was a college student. My aunt was rebuilding her life after divorce. My grandmother was a caretaker for a family in the Bronx. My grandmother and I were together again; we shared a bedroom where her rosary prayers mingled with my obsessive listening to Nina Simone. There was the constant smell of oil paint drying on the recently stretched canvas, and a tree leaned against the brick wall outside our window.

No. The home she called me back to was the home I had shared with her, her husband and their youngest son, Vincent, in Diego Martin. The home she called me back to was Trinidad and Tobago.

My motherland consists of two islands cast like emerald jewels on the mouth of the Orinoco. Off the coast of Abya Yala, which long ago was once connected to Alkebulan — these islands form an archipelago where my ancestors could, if they dared, walk all the way north to Kalaallit Nunaat. How these islands are beautiful! The colors are as vibrant as the sun is hot and the bush lush. Here, when you catch the suspended flight of the hummingbird as it darts from hibiscus to hibiscus, its long beak dipping into the flower's pistil, you know the creator spirit has your back.

My ancestors flowed out into the islands that bridge the "southern" to the "northern"; like waves of brown earth walking upon sandy shores, free. We are said to have been fierce — our warrior women are said to have worn braids. We once moved from Abya Yala, including the islands in what we call the Caribbean, subjugating and sometimes cooperating with those we encountered. We are said to have given the fiercest resistance to the Europeans, and it is after us that these islands are named. We are said to have eaten our enemies — something that may merely reflect the Europeans' compulsion to project. Now, many of us hide behind the colors of Africa and India in an attempt to make our existence less vulnerable to further exterminations.

These islands are fertilized with the blood of my people. Their blood seeps into the soil. They were the human sacrifices Europe made — for land, money, power and control. They attempt to break our souls, communities, families and land. Known initially as Kairi, this land was named by Columbus on his third voyage to the Caribbean. He named this island Trinidad, after the Holy Trinity, due to the three hills he saw in the south. In that naming is a binding, a spell, a fixing. A destiny, if people were not careful, had been cast. So that when this island was bound by the name Trinidad, this naming bound us to Europe's dreams. And us? We became the underbelly of wealth. The unhuman to their human. The chaos to their order. Tell me, *who is so bold as to think they can name the world?*

I will have many conversations with the Trinbagonian activist Gillian Goddard while I am in Trinidad. One of the things we will talk about is the issue of settlements and urban dwellings. She will explain to me the differences between how the Indigenous used this land and how the European settlers and colonists did. She will explain to me that dense settlements can only last so long, and that urban centers always eventually fall. "They don't produce anything," she tells me one day when we are "on the land." "It's not sustainable." This is something I will think deeply about, later, when I'm in Brooklyn. I will attempt to ponder the amount of concrete it takes to build a city like New York. I will ponder the smell of sour garbage in the evenings, as well as the sheer volume of people. I will ponder the fact that some subway stations look as though they have not been serviced since their inception.

"Trinidad," which before was a place where people roamed freely and set up temporary settlements so as to not overtax our surroundings, devolved into demonic plantations like Lopinot — with cruel humans whose claim to superiority is quickly challenged by the sun.

The nature of nation states is a tedious affair. By their very birth, borders violently dam what needs to move: people. The nation state is, by its very existence, a police state, damming the flow of human beings, particularly the poor. Borders, in turn, essentially cut off cultural exchanges between certain classes that historically have played a significant role in cultivating our sense of humanity and community, locally and globally. Before European countries carved up the world, granting each other large swaths of land and people, there were no visas.

Where is the court that will demand justice for the poor of the Global South?

Where are the people who see the connections between Europe's settler colonies and the destruction of not only millions of human beings but of nature herself in order to line the pockets of government officials and corporate criminals? Again, I'll ask: Where is the justice for the Indigenous of so-called Australia? The Indigenous of Turtle Island? The Black descendants of enslaved Africans all throughout the so-called Americas. The countless others whose names we do not know?

Where is the justice for all the blood spilled for the coffers of Europe?

We are the Black and Brown bodies trafficked across oceans, violently uprooted and later deemed redundant by the infrastructure of financial markets and torn from the land and people, displaced and brutalized.

We are the Black and Brown bodies, still lynched, brutalized and impoverished; Europe stole our land. We are Europe's wealth. In our deaths and imprisonment, she profits.

The very existence of the nation state impedes travel, which, when unhindered, has the potential to open up our minds and bring us closer to this earth, each other and the lives that we share. Instead, European borders and their parroting prevent the global majority's movement on this planet. Even the way we travel has been besmirched by this regime of borders, corporate infrastructures and global Western hegemony.

I would venture to say that much of our current-day problems could be traced back to the creation of the nation state, that creation which stokes great flames of patriotic passion with the same fanaticism inherent in the world of competitive sports. The nation state of Trinidad and Tobago reflects the ugly nuts and bolts of what truly fuels Europe and her settler colonies the world over. We were the darkness of Europe's so-called Enlightenment.

And like so many other human beings globally, some of us in my family have always traveled. Whether it's my grandfather's father, who migrated to Trinidad from Guyana, my great-grandmother's own family, who I only recently learned came from St. Kitts. But then there's my father's father, who is half Chinese — all of them reflecting the many different people of this world. Even my grandmother's nickname, "Hotfoot," is a testimony to how integral movement was to her.

Whenever I recall my grandmother's visits to us in Brooklyn, she rarely seemed to sit still. "They haven't named a hurricane after Hildred yet," my uncle Vince joked one day. Dressed in her white slip, she'd rummage through her grip, unwrapping clothes that held toothpaste tubes or even shampoo bottles. Then, finally, she'd throw on her stylish beige jacket, only to return to the apartment hours later, breathless and with hands full of shopping bags.

In Trinidad, she would take numerous trips to Port of Spain, coming home with early-morning market purchases of plantain, callaloo bush and other local wares. Or she might have been off to visit a sister in Santa Cruz or to attend St. John's mass — or, as the years progressed, funerals of those whose names I had only heard spoken but who I had never met. Then, of course, there were also long periods of rest and even depression.

She was of a world that experienced two wars, that experienced the Americans in Trinidad, that knew of siblings who flew fighter planes over European mountains and who vanished, never to be seen again. She walked into northern cities that she had seen on the big screen (my mother told me how my grandmother took her to the movies when she was a child. She said my grandmother was utterly entranced by the screen). With village wisdom gained in her childhood, my grandmother first sailed on boats and then flew on airplanes to faraway places, spaces that perhaps gave her some relief; relief from financial structures, relief from marriage and maybe even from parenting. She loved the glamor of city life, but would also sleep with a chamber pot under her bed — a *tensil*. She washed and reused plastic bags long before they were choking the oceans, as well as foil paper, much to my childish embarrassment as I unwrapped the wrinkly material to get to my school lunch of bake and salt fish.

Like her namesake, Hildegard of Bingen, she too, in her way, sought that which was juicy and full of life, even if it meant abandoning Caribbean shores for drafty winters.

My grandmother loved big cities and was struck by the material glitter of it all. But, with her village-girl sensibilities, she sometimes could dodge the seduction of this new world. She learned to read the intricate patterns of train maps. She'd often stand in Grand Central Station only to see the great waves of people coming and going, mesmerized by the sheer volume of it all. She got drunk from the excess of this new place; the large perfume-laden department stores where everything shone in its novelty, and the electric lights that illuminated night skies as if extending the very day itself. Other times she would succumb — intent on shipping the newest appliances and products to the family and home she left behind: a washing machine, a fridge and even televisions.

In the late Sixties, the Ministry of Labor in Trinidad and Tobago was tasked with recruiting locals to work in American homes. My grandmother always loved America — and there was no city she loved more than New York. For many like my grandmother, America was a more welcome, warmer motherland than "Great" Britain. Moreover, America is where she could permeate a less stringent class system.

Her new job would take her to the tiny world of Cumberland, Maryland. This town, nestled at the base of the Appalachian Mountains and along the banks of the Potomac River, is where my island grandmother became a migrant, in a land that would come to be known as America due to a German cartographer. It is a land whose original peoples had been conquered by the creation of borders by European settlers. A country that was founded for Whites only. A country that saw no problem planting its seeds in a land that was not its own; that believed god gave it this right to theft and murder.

"When I think about those days, I become so sad," my aunt tells me. I have only been to Trinidad for two days, and we are sitting in my favorite spot — the side of the house that faces the western mountains. My mother's younger sister, the middle one, knows everything; whenever I have a question about the family, I go to her. I had asked her how my grandmother ended up going to America. Talks about her traveling past invariably bring up her youngest son.

"When I think about how young Vincent was when she left…" My uncle Vince, the son she left behind, is six years older than me. When I lived in Trinidad, he was like my big brother, except he didn't complain about letting me tag along with him and his older friends; instead, he welcomed it.

My grandmother had given birth to my uncle at the age of forty-two. She would often reference the story of Mary's cousin, Elizabeth, who gave birth to John the Baptist late in her and her husband's life. My grandmother would refer to this biblical story when she wanted to seek some solace for the guilt she most likely felt.

By the time I had arrived in Trinidad, my grandmother had returned to the land of her birth, and her relationship with her youngest son, although full of love, was strained.

Mrs. Powell, for whom my grandmother prepared meals, was a very influential woman in her community. My grandmother found herself among folks who knew the Kennedys, who were related to a Bishop imprisoned in China. We would learn that the house where she worked was so large that there was an elevator. My grandmother was not housebound — she had a fair amount of freedom. She traveled to New York to watch the Rockettes at the Radio City Music Hall and visited her sister in D.C.; but sometimes, my aunt told me, a deep depression shook her. "I can't even eat ice cream," my grandmother said to my aunt one day. "To think my son is eating ice cream without me."

"People make different decisions in life. But me? American dollar will not make my family happier," my aunt tells me. The sun is beginning to set behind the mountains. "Imagine, I got my first real job when I was forty," my aunt continues. At the time, she says, her youngest son was seven. "I would have to leave him every morning, call him once I got to work to wake him up. And even up to the other day, I had to apologize to him," she says. Her face contorts in pain. She is a handsome woman — proud in her simplicity, humble. Sometimes she can be intimidating, but when she is warm and loving, all I want to do is be close to her.

"'Why you apologizing, mommy?' he ask me."

"I feel so bad leaving you when you were seven." His school was two houses down from where they lived. "You didn't leave me, mommy," he laughed, "you had to go to work."

"If I left my children," my aunt says, "like Mummy had wanted me to do, then I would have missed out on my children in their formative years. American dollar not worth that. Parents have to be mindful of their duties," she tells me. In the narrative arcs of motherhood in my family, she is indeed the only mother who stayed. She is the only mother who enjoys a rich and full relationship with her children. "All the money made in America didn't change a thing in Mummy's life. Me and my husband, we poor. We have no money. But we never regret it."

2.

My motherland
has a border

When I land in Trinidad, disembark and enter the airport and am surrounded mainly by other Trinbagonians, I know that I am home. I feel a landing of my soul I have not felt since the last time I was here. Everyone around me looks and sounds familiar. The palm trees and balmy heat nourish my soul. The early morning sky is stretched above the mountains, lavender with salmon-colored ribbon-like clouds. I am humbled by how beautiful my mother's country is.

But when I arrive at the border of Trinidad and Tobago, I am confronted with the harsh realities of what it can sometimes mean to enter nation states. This landing is the first time I have landed at Piarco International Airport in almost ten years. It is not the same airport composed of a wooden shack Naipaul once described (far from it). It is not the same Piarco that greeted me in the early Eighties when I was a child arriving from Brooklyn to live with my grandparents. No, it was now a much larger and modern one.

There was air conditioning everywhere and a more modern indoor shopping center with stores that sold items intended to reflect the soul of the place: T-shirts and coasters with the symbols that have come to depict Trinbagonian's nationalism; our black-white-and-red flag; images of hummingbirds suspended in flight and of the scarlet ibis; depictions of dark brown bodies, colorful outfits in limbo and bright hibiscus flowers painted onto coffee mugs. Global franchises fill the airport, while many local merchants are left outside.

Even though the twin-island nation of Trinidad and Tobago is the birthplace of both my parents, and I have been there many more times than I can count, this is the border where I experience the most tension. Not in Europe or the States — but in Trinidad and Tobago, and not for the first time. The last time I came to Trinidad, I was with my son, who was eight years old. I handed over my passport to the officer, eager to leave and meet up with Vince, who had come to pick us up from the airport. Instead, the officer took my passport, checked it on the computer and then looked up at me. She then looked into the computer screen again.

"Can you wait one second, please?" she asked as she stepped away from her desk and went to the back office. My son and I looked at each other. What was that?

She returned shortly after, took her seat, stamped my passport and handed it to me. "Sorry about that, here you go. Welcome to Trinidad and Tobago."

As I was about to take my passport and walk away, I decided to ask. "Could you tell me what that was about?"

"Well, there's a Lesley-Ann Brown on our watchlist." Then she looked at my son and then back at me, "But we don't think it's you. So there must be another Lesley-Ann Brown."

Now I was again experiencing tension at the border.

"How long are you staying?" the officer asked me, although the return date is on the ticket. In fact, as a non-citizen, I would not be allowed into the country if I did not have a return ticket. She is not warm or welcoming.

I politely answer, to which she responds, "And what is the purpose of your visit?"

I explain that I am there to bury my dead grandmother.

"Are you married?" she asks me.

"Excuse me?" I ask. "What does my marital status have to do with anything?"

"Well, you never know what kind of business you coming here for," she continued. "There's a lot of prostitutes trying to come here."

Welcome to Trinidad and Tobago.

The land of your ancestors thinks you are a whore. I remember long ago when I had to tell Hussain, one of my first students, a sixth grader, that he was never to call any of his classmates a whore under any uncertain terms.

"But why?" he asked, his face fresh like a newly blossomed flower. He seemed so innocent, and he was. "What is a whore?" he asked. That's when I realized that, although the kids used the word all the time, they had no idea what it was. It was kind of hilarious if you think about it. At that time, I taught at a private school with primarily Muslim students run by a loud-mouthed Canadian who claimed he looked like Al Pacino.

"It's someone who sells themselves for money," I told him.

"But Lesley," my sweet sixth grader said, "everyone does that."

It was at this school where I first met some of the world: students whose identities on the other side of the hyphen were Pakistani, like Sami, Palestinian, like Bilal, Lebanese, like Hussain, Egyptian, like Abdullah, Turkish, like Linda, Somali, like Zanubia, Iranian, like Parsa and Iraqi, like Jumana. Like kids everywhere, they came up with creative insults, which revealed their own hierarchies: "stateless" for the Palestinians, "Kurd" for the Kurdish students and *perker* — a Danish derogatory word for foreigners, mostly Muslims, which they embraced and called each other by like their own personal "n" word. The Danish kids were called potatoes, although I tried to tell them that potatoes were originally from South America.

There is something about the way Trinidadians speak that entrances me. Like all other dialects, the Trinbagonian lilt is our way of indigenizing English. To enunciate each word is not economical — especially when it is a language that has historically been a tool of oppression. "Speak proper English!" someone would say derisively, usually to distance themselves from what they perceive as common. There are different iterations, of course, depending on who the person sees themselves as or based on the particular geographic area. Still to this day, hearing my mother say my name, with the Trinidadian country accent she has managed to maintain over the fifty years she has lived in Brooklyn, is like feeling the ocean breeze across sunburnt cheeks.

It's times like this, when I hear the voices of Trinbagonians, that I long after my own authentic voice — my mother tongue. I once spoke as if I sang from my heart, but like Hans Christensen's foolish mermaid, I gave up my voice. When I returned to Brooklyn as a fifteen-year-old, I grew weary whenever someone stopped what I was saying to ask me about my accent. Already marginalized as a young Black girl, I took my accent and buried it deep within my heart. It sometimes escapes, sometimes in anger, sometimes when I am in a condition of immense ease. But it is not something I can call up and switch on like so many others have learned to do. I grieve over its loss and hope that one day it will be the only tongue in which I speak.

Like so many other times before, I am met at the airport by my uncle Vincent, and we embrace. He still looks the same, except he has gained a little weight on what used to be a skinny frame, and his hair is much shorter than how he used to wear it before, in a high Afro.

"How are you doing, Las-lay?" he asks me in his fake American accent.

The gorgeous green hills greeted me as they always have. Lord only knows how often I have come and gone from this airport. As we began the drive to Diamond Vale, I sat back and marveled at the beauty around me, wondering why did I ever leave?

I love Trinidad and Tobago — not as a nation state but as a geographic location, its tropical topography a resistance, the bush remembering what we cannot. No matter where you look — from former sugar plantations to concrete houses, the power of the bush will be witnessed. Like the heat of the sun, it cannot be tamed. No matter if specific demographics in Trinidad strive toward a more North-American, European lifestyle, the bush will always reclaim, spreading like wildfire.

When I'm in Trinidad, I sometimes close my eyes and imagine what this land felt and looked like before nation-binding. I smell the land before me, the earth seemingly still fresh despite its history. I touch the foliage of plants around me, the crotons that take me back to my grandmother's garden, caring not for its name but only that it could have been a plant once touched by my ancestors. I like that I could feel I'm in a space my ancestors once inhabited. That my great-grandmother on my father's side was Carib — or Kalinago — only deepens this connection. I have a lineage in that locality that stretches back long before the project of modernity. This lineage connects me to the land mass "below" — Abya Yala — and to the Amazon, although I've never been. I understand it may be easy for me to fantasize about a romantic idea I have of my Abya Yala homeland, but how can I make this present by being mindful of my current surroundings? Be they Brooklyn, Oakland, Copenhagen or even Trinidad? The point is that I want to feel deeply connected to all of the earth, not just to locations where I may have a personal bond. So when I travel, I seek out those things that brush upon my memories, reignite them and keep me connected. I pay attention to the trees and the plants that grow between the concrete. I listen to the birdsong in the Danish countryside and imagine it is a rainforest near the equator. I walk barefoot on the grass, allowing my feet freedom that shoes do not permit. In the evenings, if possible, I train my eyes at the sky and marvel at this beautiful planet we have been so fortunate to inherit.

It makes sense that, for the first time in over ten years, my maternal grandmother, Hildred Balbirsingh, makes me return to the land of my mothers. It also makes sense that her funeral will coincide with the world-renowned national Trinbagonian ritual of Carnival.

In Christianshavn, a once working-class town, now gentrified area of Copenhagen, I met a white-haired Danish woman. She had lived in the southern town of San Fernando, Trinidad, with her husband, who worked in the oil business. We sat and chatted about her time there, drinking coffee and eating cake. Then she said, "I just thought there would have been more culture there, but it all seemed like everywhere else."

I didn't then and still don't agree with her. But I understood what she meant — she wanted something to "discover," something not many other Europeans would have access to. Although superficially Trinidad and Tobago has most of the sites that one must have as a Western country — malls, movie theaters, suburban houses and Kentucky Fried Chicken — there is much that harkens back to the cultures of many of our ancestors. Take, for instance, Carnival, a festival once celebrated by the French colonists and which excluded the enslaved; it is this island nation's ultimate expression of creativity, roots, *routes* and letting go.

Carnival in Trinidad is *bacchanal* — a time to party, play old mas' and engage with passions before the great national cleanse — Lent. It is a time to don skimpy costumes, whine up your waist and get on bad. It's when every song is a tune — the ability to be in the joyful moment. With rhythms inherited from our motherland, Africa, music becomes liberating.

During my trip, I have the opportunity to meet the celebrated author Earl Lovelace. The activist Gillian Goddard, who will take me under her care, takes me over to his house alongside a wooded ravine. There, he will remark that everything distinctly Trinidadian — like pan, limbo, Carnival even — is Black. "We have Chinese events, Syrian, Indian — but whenever it has to do with Black culture? We call it Trinidadian," he complained.

We are our ancestors' ability to transform and be magic when we partake. Our ability to survive historical atrocities becomes culture: Oshun and steel drums, truth-saying and soca, Rasta, resistance, calypso and stick-fighting; moko jumbos and limbo.

Those of us who answer the call to hit the concrete and play mas' follow trucks blasting soca and calypso and the many hybrids we have created, chipping down the road. Sometimes we rub up on each other — we answer the call with complete abandon, bringing the entire nation to a halt with one goal allowed: Bacchanal.

Officially, carnival is two days, but I can attest that Carnival festivities start to gear up right after Christmas. In other words, technically, some party all year.

While many invest in expensive costumes produced by legendary bands, I've always reveled in being a free agent. So me and my crew take a maxi taxi into town and jump up with whoever we want, going from band to band, partaking in the festivities. Hot sun, loud music and bright colors are as varied as the many fabrics. Bodies are on display, and even though I may not be wearing a costume, that won't stop me from crossing the stage at the Savannah with a band (should I find yourself in such a situation).

My first mas' was with Burrokeets — an ole' mas' band whose costume consisted of crocus bags and mud. It was Jouvet morning — that moment when carnival bursts onto the streets from the dark early morning along with the rising sun. Vat 19, a Trinidadian rum company, sponsored the band — so the spirits flowed throughout the day. I was thirteen.

Ole' mas' is about freedom — all it takes is a little creativity to access it. So we — my mother's youngest sister, her friend Dianne and I — happily chipped our way through Port of Spain, passing through hordes of people, jumping up and whining under the blazing sun, participating in a ritual that our ancestors indigenized. And we danced.

I've always loved to dance. Pat was a parent in the Brooklyn building I lived in on Ocean Avenue. She would often take all the kids roller-skating or bowling. I suspected she did this because her oldest son, just sixteen, was the first in the building to be locked up at New York City's infamous Rikers Island. Stanley was a beautiful boy who wore silky durags, an impeccable crease running down the front and back of each denim pant leg, the pants' waist hanging just below his belly button.

I suspect Pat did not want her younger son, Curtis, who would blow me kisses from his bedroom window, or any of us, for that matter, to get distracted by the streets. So she would take us, a large group of kids whose parents hailed from the African diaspora — the American South, Guyana, Jamaica, Panama, Trinidad — on the bus from Ocean Avenue to Empire Roller Disco on Empire Boulevard and Flatbush. After hours of skating, we'd return to our sneakers and hit the center of the rink, where we danced to songs like Lisa Lisa & Cult Jam's "Can You Feel the Beat," Tom Tom Club's "Genius of Love" and Rick James's "Super Freak." This was before I moved to Trinidad.

In Trinidad, party life includes liming — that word that captures the art of hanging out, exchanging stories, laughing, debating and drinking — discussing local politics, drinking rum and coke and eating. My uncle Vince took me everywhere with him to lime: to the mall, Regatta, into town. This meant I was that twelve-year-old at Pelican Bar, smoking Du Muriers, drinking Carib and believing I was grown. We'd sit in pubs that played Zeppelin's "Stairway to Heaven" or rum shops that blared Billy Paul's "Me and Mrs. Jones." Between doing our best to imitate the lives of our North American neighbors in music videos and movies, we had the best of both worlds and reveled in our own party culture, which was rooted in community and release. We limed on beautiful beaches, hitched rides on fishing boats to get out to *down de islands* and hiked through the mountains and their bush from Arima to Maracas.

"Five days of carnival is too much bacchanal, in Trinidad, in Trinidad!" was the refrain from a popular calypso the year I arrived in Trinidad as a ten-year-old. But now, I am in no mood to party, I'm here to bury my grandmother. And her funeral will happen six days before my forty-sixth birthday, which also happens to be her own mother's birthday.

The funeral is tomorrow.

I would have never imagined that I would be able to be with my grandmother as she passed from this life. Although my soul always points toward the island of my foremothers, returning to Trinidad wasn't a reality I felt I was near fulfilling when I left Denmark just two months before. First of all, I didn't have the contacts. I hadn't lived in Trinidad since the Eighties and knew very little about the present community. I still had childhood friends there — but I remain an anomaly among them. While they all have gone on to marry and have families and continue the weekly ritual of attending mass, I have eschewed this lifestyle. And my own family was fragmented — throughout the years, some of us grew further and further apart, primarily due to migrations and lifestyles. That the universe conspired for me to be with my grandmother when she transitioned, to be back in Trinidad for her funeral, my birthday and during Carnival, further deepens my belief that there are higher powers.

3.

My grandmother
is Trinidad

When I arrived in Trinidad, I gushed to my uncle Vince, "I see Mummy Hildred everywhere!" I heard her in the melodic tone of Trinbagonians, in the utterance of geographic names such as Blanchisseuse; I saw her in the mountains of the northern range, in the flaming flamboyant tree that she'd often point out to me, teaching me about the natural world I had landed in as a child. My grandmother was everywhere.

"What happen' to you?" My uncle sucks his teeth and has his arms akimbo. "That devil talk, gyul!" No matter how much time I spend with my uncle, nothing will ever prepare me for the level of religiosity he sometimes expresses. One minute he's the gregarious uncle I had known as a child, reminiscing about our Eighties youth, and the next he is explaining to me why Black people are the original Israelites. "Anyone reading the bible knows that it's about Black people," he says. He now explains to me, "Mummy gone, gyul. She gone. Anything else is devil talk." I will later learn that he also believes yoga and meditation to be devilish pursuits, despite our multiple lineages that point back to India, not least my family's name.

According to him, I am not to believe that my grandmother is still on this plane in any shape or form. But after I arrive in Trinidad, I feel nothing but my grandmother, see nothing but my grandmother, hear nothing but my grandmother — my grandmother is Trinidad. Trinidad is my grandmother

***

My grandmother was raised by Nen-nen, an Afro-Trinidadian woman who took care of the local church. She only spent a few years with her other three sisters and her parents. "I know what it's like to not live with your family," she told me one day, not too long after I had arrived in Trinidad as a child. She sat in the wicker rocking chair on the gallery, a bowl of long, emerald *bodi* on her lap, which she snapped into two-inch parts and placed in the pot beside her. I loved to watch how expertly she seemed to do everything, from scrubbing clothes on the washboard to making green seasoning, the scent of ginger and *shado beni* spicy and full of life. I enjoyed the scent of blue soap and how the water transformed into suds of ivory. She wore her brown house dress, and her curly hair was cut short. Her legs were strong and her back straight.

My grandmother's experience embedded in her a deep empathy for the ostracized, something I would witness time and time again as a child living with her, from her taking me in as a precocious Brooklyn girl to opening our home for extended stays to Wendell, a blind student, or Sharmane, a sixteen-year-old from Arima whose pregnancy significantly disrupted her family's church-going aspirations. Sharmane would tell me how she would let her lover into her room at night through her window. She seemed determined not to follow her family in their religious ways.

It was my grandmother who told me about my childhood. "You used to speak patois — like the Haitians," she'd say to me. "And no one understood you but me, because your great-grandmother, my mother, spoke patois." Patois could mean many things throughout the Caribbean, but in this case, my grandmother was talking about French creole. Her mother had worked on a cocoa plantation connected to France by Corsica. In Trinidad, there were first the Caribs and Arawaks, then the Spanish, the British and other Europeans, along with the souls they dragged across the Atlantic and the Indian Ocean. As a result, to be in Trinidad is to hear these languages, whether in the names of places or embedded in our language: Cocorite, Maracas, Carenage, Arima, Sangre Grande. Our creolization of language includes words from Africa, India and the Indigenous.

After the Haitian Revolution, many other colonies on neighboring islands offered free land to lure the plantation class who fled the specter of the formerly enslaved demanding equality, liberty and fraternity (a truer revolution than France's could ever be). That my first words were in the language of these Haitian liberators always fills me with a feeling of purpose.

Ever since I was a child, I remember my grandmother telling me I shared the same birthday as her mother. "And you look like her too," she'd say. "Your face jokey just like hers," she'd continue, looking at me, a slight smile on her face, letting me know that she was teasing. I always felt that my grandmother respected me, no matter how differently I lived my life from her. In many ways, I thought that she looked at my life with some distant awe — as if I was living an alternate life she could have had if she had been born in another time. She was delighted about my good grades, and since I did so well in school, she entrusted me in my uncle Vincent's care, giving me a lot of freedom. Other times, she'd tell me that I looked like Penny., "Maybe you can be the next Ms. Universe," she'd tell me, referring to our island's first Ms. Universe, who would end up being the first Black Ms. Universe ever in 1977. Ms. Janelle Penny Commissiong, as beautiful as she is, was always a bane in my side. "Why would you want me to walk on stage with a bathing suit?" I'd answer my grandmother. No insult to Ms. Commissiong — but I was never into beauty pageants. I was too busy reading.

We fought, especially when I was a young teenager living with her in Trinidad. But for the most part we were in harmony; together, our very breaths became synchronized, creating a space of safety I desperately needed. I loved helping clean — scrubbing the bathroom tiles, sweeping and mopping floors — it made her happy and made me feel good to be of service to her.

I remember, however, when it dawned on me that I would not return to Brooklyn and my mother. I felt resentment toward my grandmother — in my childish mind, I thought of her extreme care for me as something that was even keeping me away from my mother. Of course, nothing could have been further from the truth, but I had never had anyone mother me the way my grandmother did. I had never had anyone parent me with such love. I remember, once, she showed up at Providence Girls' Catholic School out of breath and with a look of worry on her face. School was over and I was liming in the parking lot with some friends. I was surprised to see her.

"There's a parent-teacher meeting?" she asked, looking around, confused. I was confused too. No one in my family had ever shown up to school for me. And here she was.

And while my grandmother had been married, most likely faithfully, to my grandfather since she was eighteen, my dating habits were very different. First of all, I have always been obsessed with falling in love. I started to develop crushes relatively young and enjoyed getting lost in my head in scenes that removed me far from reality. From as far back as I remember, I always had crushes — Dexter, Armandito, Sean, Jesus — all beautiful boys from Brooklyn reflecting the world. Getting lost in my imagination was a way for me to cope with the chaos of my home life in Brooklyn.

In Trinidad, these delusions were further fueled by cheap paperback romance novels that my slightly older cousin always consumed. I learned to escape my yearnings for my mother, who was back in Brooklyn, and to salve the pain of this loss by fixating on "love." I "fell in love" with boys like Marlon West, who went to Queens Royal College and would come by my primary school at the end of the day, or Ricky, the Chinese boy who lived down the street from me who went to St. Anthony's. Finally, there was Robert Cyril, a green-eyed Indian boy who lived in the village of Patna.

Throughout the years I lived with my grandparents, my grandmother often confronted me with rumors people brought to her. I was always amused by the creative retellings that came back to me. There was the one about an older Swedish man whose hotel room she had heard I had gone to. Now, I was wild, but going back to a hotel room with someone was way outside of anything even I would do! The most I did was to take off with someone; that's when you'd couple up. To kiss. And I loved it. I was starved for physical contact. I now understand my desire for physical connection, couple with my clinginess, as being the result of not having a physically intimate family. Once, when I was about nine and back in Brooklyn, I attempted to stroke my father's arm with love. "What 'you doing?" He grabbed his arm away from me, an amused and surprised look on his face. He sucked his teeth and shook his head as though a daughter touching her father was strange.

But the Swedish man?

It was in the early Eighties, Carnival time, and Vince, Gillian (his form-five classmate), her brother Dereck and I decided to go into town. Free agents. We hopped on a maxi taxi that played calypso so loud we had to scream when we spoke to each other, and made our way into town. Once there, we jumped out of the maxi taxi. The streets were not fully packed, but the sound of calypso and soca could be heard coming from giant speakers all around. The hot sun, loud music and general raucous vibe were liberating. Everybody seemed to be enthralled in the joyous release. We walked on the savannah, the part where the stage was located as little clouds of dust covered our sneakers. We had a flask of rum, stolen from the supermarket, to which we added cola. The hot sun was *lashin'* — it beat down on our skin as we drank and smoked cigarettes. While walking around Woodbrook, we saw this giant blond guy lying face down in the middle of the street. He looked so vulnerable — his skin pink from the sun, his wallet sticking out of his back pocket. We went over to him.

"What the ass happen to this man?" my uncle Vince asked, arms akimbo, a loud sucking of his teeth escaping his mouth. "You see? When something happens to him, he will say Trinis fuck up. How you going to go to somebody's country and pass out in the middle of the people street?" He had a point. I leaned over and took the wallet that was sticking out of his back pocket. I didn't recognize the language, but before I could investigate further, he groaned and rolled over unto his back.

"Hi," he said, a smile cracking his red, sunburnt face. We all stood there, peering down at him. He sat up. And this is how we met Helman, a Swedish postman who was visiting Trinidad for his first Carnival. Helman was very drunk.

Helman was so drunk that he couldn't walk. We decided to take him back to his hotel.

Somehow, someone saw us taking Helman back to his hotel — but told my grandmother the story in such a way that it suggested it was just this man and me.

Whenever I corrected these rumors for my grandmother, she always believed me. Always shy of emotionally intimate relationships, I developed a relationship with her that I had been unable or unwilling to form with others. This was primarily because my grandmother consistently demonstrated trust and loyalty to me, which I found empowering. It was as if she wanted me to be fully who I was. And that made me respect her. Because she respected me, despite how vastly different we were.

When we later shared a bedroom in an apartment in Brooklyn, she asked me, "Do you enjoy sex?" It was the early Nineties; I had just started college and was running to and from Manhattan, usually in jean cut-offs, tights and boots. Even in the winter. Like all other youths in New York, I was young and thought myself eternal. Hiding nothing, my aunt and grandmother would witness the phone calls, the dates and the nights not spent at home. "Of course," I answered, smiling as I zipped up my patent-leather go-go boots. This was during the time when Tompkins Square Park was being violently emptied and Giuliani's policies included criminalizing the mentally insane to make way for a more economically cut-throat city. In the early Nineties, New York was Polish bars, pool halls, Continental Divide, the Wah Wah Hut, Pyramid Club, Limelight and Mars. Crack and police brutality.

She studied me for a minute — a smile tugging at her lips. "You enjoy your life, gyul," she said to me, sucking on a tamarind ball. "You're smart. You'll figure it out. But me? I never did enjoy it."

To my childhood friends, I am an anomaly: I am twice divorced, single and seem to travel a lot. We have very little in common anymore, except our memories of growing up in a country that was the perfect backdrop to adolescent adventures. I go to the Maracas with one crew, receive another at the house and even go out to dinner with a few others.

After the niceties of meeting and catching up, I was alone in the house in Diamond Vale with my two uncles. It was perhaps one of the loneliest moments in my life.

When I had just arrived in Trinidad as a ten-year-old and saw my grandmother among the crowd awaiting their friends, family or lovers coming from New York, my first thought was that she had aged. I was ten, raised mainly in Brooklyn, the borough of my birth, and I had mostly only seen my grandmother when she visited us on her many trips there. Back then, she didn't have a lot of gray hair, but she'd pay me five cents for each I could pull out. This time, however, she had a headful.

I'm not sure what it was about this that made me feel sad. Maybe I was unconsciously dealing with the fact that I was no longer under the care of my mother and that this woman would be who would have to parent me for however long I stayed. The truth is, the only thing I knew was that I was going to live with my grandmother in Trinidad — no one explained to me what that would entail, such as being far away from my mother, or that the school system was different and that I would rarely be able to go back and visit my family in Brooklyn.

By then, that home was falling apart. My sister, only sixteen, had already run away. I'll never forget the day she came home and asked me to throw her duffel bag down to her from our bedroom window. By this time, she had decided that she no longer wanted to live in the chaos that was our family home. I had wanted to go with her, and was disappointed when she said no. Once she had gone, I stuck my head out the window to make sure she was there — we were on the sixth floor and it took her a while to get downstairs. I threw her bag down to her, and as her bag landed on the ground, I heard the sound of a can of hairspray as it fell out and rolled onto the pavement. I rarely saw my brother, who moved out not too long after I left for Trinidad.

Upon seeing my grandmother at the airport and how much she had aged, I felt sad. Sad that I had been sent to Trinidad to live (although it was the best thing that could have happened to me!); sad that she had gotten older without me. But I was happy to see her, and she was delighted to see me. We embraced; her smell of flowery cream reminded me of the many times I'd crawled into her lap as a younger child, secure in her love and attention.

The first thing I noticed after disembarking from the airplane was a loud chorus of chirps. I couldn't place the sound, although it was everywhere — seeming to drown out all other noise, including the airplanes landing and taking off.

"What is that noise?" I asked my grandmother, confused.

"What noise?"

"The loud chirping?" I couldn't place the sound. I had never heard it before.

"It's the frogs," she told me. If she had told me that there would be a time when the noise would fall to the background and become as natural as the air I breathe, I would have never believed her.

On our way back to Diamond Vale in Diego Martin, my grandmother told Peterson, the neighbor who had volunteered to take her to the airport to pick me up, "Le' we take she up to

Mt. St. Benedict, nah." We had to drive past the capital city of Port of Spain, and she wanted to show me how the city looked from up high in the hills. We all piled out of the car, and I saw the expanse of the island that would be my home for the next four years. In the night sky, the valleys below were illuminated by the moving car lights, enchanting those of us who could see. I didn't know it then, but coming to Trinidad was the best thing I could have done.

Back in Brooklyn, my life had fallen apart. Although only ten, I was desperate for a new beginning. School life had progressively deteriorated along with home life. Back in Brooklyn, I didn't feel safe at school anymore. Although the school was the only place I had ever experienced any structure in my life, that had changed due to the high level of fighting some of us were engaged in. So, rather than go to school, I started ditching it altogether, often walking straight past the school many mornings. I would walk from Midwood to Hudde Junior High — through Brooklyn's segregated streets, past the Victorian homes of my Flatbush neighborhood. When I did attend school, I started hanging out with the kids from the other classes. I suddenly began to feel my IGC class — intelligent, gifted children — was too elitist. My reasoning went a little like this: Why do I want to be in a system that disregarded me and so many others? Why were classes segregated by "intelligence"? Why was I in a class segregated from the others? And to me, the other kids seemed so much more enjoyable.

Tobacco Nicotiana
Used for dressing wounds and
reducing pain
Ceremonial Plant

Nicotiana tabacum L.

By now, I had developed a habit of talking my mother into things that she should never have been talked into but which, probably due to sheer exhaustion, she always did. When I was twelve, for example, I told her that I smoked and wanted her to know because I didn't want to do it behind her back. She said okay. The truth is, I had already started smoking. Although I wasn't inhaling, I would smoke in my school bathroom. Finally, it became so bad that the school's principal once requested that I smoke outside. I was in the fourth grade. My mother agreed to my smoking but said she didn't want me to smoke in front of her. At this time, I unconsciously believed that smoking meant that I was grown. I wanted to grow up.

Being a child sucked. No one explained anything to me. No one protected me. No one guided me. I foolishly thought if I was to be on my own, I at least should be able to sail my ship.

Lately, I've been paying attention to my relationship with tobacco. As my interest in plant medicine grew, I wondered about this attachment I have had with this plant. According to Monica Gagliano, cited previously in my ayahuasca chapter, tobacco is considered to be the grandfather of plant medicine. There's a difference between the tobacco used in ceremony and the one that we smoke commercially, of course, but I thought it interesting when she shared that tobacco was traditionally used to treat grief.

Grief. That feeling of deep sorrow that we feel, usually in connection to loss. When I look back to when I first started smoking as a child — there were great feelings of grief that I felt but had no way to process it.

The first time I realized it was easy to talk my mother into doing something was when, one day in the fifth grade, I said, "I don't want to be in an IGC class anymore." She stood at the kitchen counter kneading the dough for bake. She wore her usual flower-print house dress, which flowed down to her ankles. Her hair was in rows of large pink rollers, tied tightly under a silk scarf. Her eyebrows were pressed together, a look of seriousness on her face. I had started at this school in second grade, but neither of my parents had ever attended a parent-teacher meeting. My mother would show up on my birthdays with cake and ice cream, and I remember her accompanying us on a school trip. I know she did her best, given the circumstances. Although my parents praised me for my academic performance at school, looking back now I can see that they (much like my grandparents when I lived with them) didn't know what to do with it. Like so many other children — before, since and after — I had to figure it out as I went along. I wasn't doing a great job; I was, after all, only a child. But children see things clearly: I noticed that my mother was always tired and my father frustrated; that my sister and father did not get along; that my brother was running the streets. My parents would sometimes criticize American culture — for its superficiality and stupidity. Still, they never took the time to try to understand the needs of the three children who were under their care. I don't think this was a conscious decision on their part but rather a result of their fractured childhoods and their relationship with their parents as well.

The kitchen, messy from use, still smelled like the yellow onions my mother had sliced for the smoked herring we'd have with the bake once it was roasted.

"What do you mean?" my mother asked absently as she drizzled more flour on the dough. She worked most evenings, and the only time I seemed to see her was between shifts, when she was sleeping or tending to the house as best as she could.

"I don't want to be in a special class anymore. I don't believe that we should be separated in that way." I had thought about the argument before bringing it to her. "I don't think it's okay to give some students special privileges over others," I told her. And that was true. I did believe these things. And again, the kids in the other classes were way more interesting.

There was Poochie, who was all round — his cheeks, his Afro, his shape — and Kenyatta, who, along with Poochie, could always be found on the handball court, fluttering back and forth like some urban butterfly. There was Makeba, who I had known because my mother would let her and her family — Jehovah's Witnesses — into the apartment. She only did that when my father wasn't there. Then there was Rosa Martinez, a black-haired Puerto Rican with whom I had recently started hanging out. She had her period, which I thought was the most fascinating thing ever. These were the kids I wanted to spend my time with at school. The other kids, the kids in my class, weren't me. They were straight, and I was wayward. Surprisingly, my mother agreed and even came to school to speak to the principal. I was soon released from my class and placed in another class.

The fighting drove my parents to send me to Trinidad in the end. Of course, not all the kids in the school fought — but it was a way certain things were established. Take, for example, Dexter Morris: I had been in class with him since the second grade and was madly in love with him since first laying eyes on him. His dark-brown oval face was painted with the most delicate features — large brown eyes with luscious lashes; his hair was always seemingly freshly cut. He wore all the freshest clothes, from his black-on-white Adidas to his white-and-blue-suede Pumas. Like most other kids at my school, at least those whose parents could afford it, he was dressed well daily. This was not the case with me.

But I barely spoke to Dexter. He had a mean demeanor, and everyone was afraid of him. Then, one day, Poochie and Kenyatta jumped him. And the next day? Dexter Morris was a changed boy. I had never and still have not seen a transformation as powerful as that.

In Brooklyn, you had to protect yourself from bullies. If someone came at you, you couldn't back off. It didn't matter if that person was going to kick your ass. You had to fight. I learned all of these things from my friend Tracy, my round-faced best friend who was in love with Magic Johnson and always had a crown of beaded braids, in various patterns, falling over her big black eyes. I'm not sure why Tracy befriended me, but to this day I associate it with a deep sense of kindness on her part.

Around that time, my arch enemy was Toshiba, who was once my best friend. She had just arrived in my fourth-grade class, and I could recognize myself in her tattered and too-big clothes. Toshiba's hair was unkempt — she was not like the other kids in my class. She lived right around the corner from me, on East 21st Street, her large family living in a dilapidated house. Her family were five-percenters, and her father, who worked for Transit, played the saxophone. He would even come over to jam with my father, who played the organ. Toshiba and I often exchanged books: *A Hero Ain't Nothing but a Sandwich; Are You there God? It's Me, Margaret?* by Alice Childress and Judy Blume respectively. Like me, Toshiba was a poor Black girl doing her best in this world.

Sometimes we'd cut school together. We'd squat in her backyard among broken bikes and old kitchen appliances, counting coins we'd stolen from our parents — from my father's jeans pockets or my mother's dressing table among her perfume bottles and tubes of lipstick. After we tallied the money, we'd walk from her house on East 21st to Flatbush, not along Glenwood but through the quieter, more residential roads along Brooklyn College. Once at the store, we'd buy packs of Now & Laters that would stain our tongues red, beef jerky and Bubblicious. We'd walk back to school when it was over, toward the bustling, newly released students, a wire double-Dutch rope tucked snugly under one of our arms.

And double Dutch was our jam. Our feet drumming the pavements, our voices syncopated:

Jack be nimble,
Jack be quick,
Jack jump over the candlestick.

Perfecting our pop-ups, the way our bodies moved with the rhythm of the ropes, all of us, turners, jumpers and spectators, were transported by this magical performance. Playing double Dutch didn't require any money — all I had to do was chase down a Bell Telephone truck and ask a service guy for some cable. If I was lucky, which I was all the time, I would get a generous supply to last until the white surface gradually wore down to its wire core.

Toshiba's appearance was as untidy as mine. I remember when she first started in our fourth-grade class; I spied that her shoes were lacquered with a pearly gold nail polish. I remember my soul aghast in horror — it looked so terrible. Then I looked down at my appearance and noticed I wasn't far from where she was: I had a forest-green cardigan that only sported one leather button and which was a tad too small. But it was my favorite sweater and was the one I had worn when I got chosen by David from *Sesame Street* to come up on the stage in front of the whole school and be asked my name. "Lesley," I whispered shyly into the mic, my head trained on my little fingers, which attempted to wring some security from the loose leather button. But, of course, I hadn't expected to be chosen. I had wildly shot my arm up, like all the others around me in the auditorium. "Me! Me!" I yelled until he stopped right in front of me, grabbed me by my little hands and led me to the stage. And it was David! David was probably every Brooklyn child's first crush!

David reminded me of my father and many men I grew up seeing. He was one of the few Black men on television, and not just any television: PBS! Where my other favorite show, *Mr. Roger's Neighborhood*, aired. It was the first time I had ever been on stage, and I remember feeling terror through my little third-grade body, mingled with excitement.

I wasn't a good fighter. So when my and Toshiba's love finally distilled into heavy hate, I'd come home with scratches all over my face and patches of hair gone. But even back then, I knew why she and I fought: we were almost the perfect reflection of each other. I sometimes wonder about Toshiba. She was fierce and intelligent. She stayed in the IGC class long after my departure.

When I heard that a group of girls was planning to jump me, I did what any other hood girl would do — I took a razor blade to school. My fighting eventually led to my parents sending me "down there," to what they called "home."

When we pulled into the driveway of my grandparent's house in Diamond Vale, it was dark, so I couldn't see much. I was greeted by my aunty Bernice and her three children, who flanked her in the dimly lit garage at the side of the gallery. My grandmother had large, white clay pots for ferns and a variety of other tropical plants with large leaves along the gallery. I could still hear the loud chirping and my grandfather watching the evening news, *Panorama*, when we entered the house. In those days, there was only one television channel in Trinidad, and I look back on those days fondly. He looked up and, when he saw me, stood up.

A large smile pierced his dark face. He wore an orange tank top and shorts, his feet in Bata slippers. "Well, well, well," he said. I always liked my grandfather, but my Americanness drove him crazy. He smiled and returned to his tan-leather reclining chair, the one he would later go on to allow my cat to sleep on, declaring, "Eh eh, you ain't see how Pussin' take my seat?" A laugh flowed from his mouth. By the time I left Trinidad, I had two cats, and both of them, no matter what I named them, were called Pussin' by him, and Pussin' they became.

My grandmother was busy bustling all about me, showing me the living room, its wooden dining table, a couple of wicker chairs and the leather recliner. There was a fan blowing warm air. The kitchen was narrow and led out to the washroom and backyard. Next to the kitchen was granddaddy's bedroom, and next to that, Vincent's. Across from Vincent's room was my grandmother's. Her bed was nicely made. Her windows were louvers that were placed high, close to the ceiling, so passersby could not look into the house. The gallery was right outside her window. She had a chest of drawers with prayer books, rosaries and various powders and lipsticks on the lace-covered top. "You must be tired," she said.

"You'll be sleeping with me," she told me. It didn't seem unusual to sleep there, as I slept most nights in my parents' bed, only for my father to carry me into my bed while I slept when he came home from his graveyard shift. I changed into my nightgown and got into bed. I woke up in the middle of the night and found my grandmother sleeping, snoring beside me. A faint light came through her street window, casting the shadow of her sheer curtains across her face and against the wall. What was this strange new world I had conjured up for myself? What was this place? Who were these people? And importantly, when was I going back home to my parents?

4.

Adventures of
a force-ripe fruit

When I came to Trinidad to live as a ten-year-old, my grandmother signed me up at Diamond Vale Government Primary School. I remember the day we walked under the sweltering sun from our home in the old vale on Emerald Drive, across what was once Diamond Vale Boulevard, to Diamond Vale Government Primary School on Aquamarine Drive in the new vale. It was so hot that my grandmother stopped and asked an elderly brown woman sitting in her gallery for a glass of water. The lady's face broke into a smile when she saw us. "Is hot the sun hot today!" I was surprised at how warmly she received us and the swiftness with which my grandmother and this woman fell into a lively banter that covered everything from politics to the weather and the economy. It was 1982, the entire world was experiencing an economic "crisis," and in Trinidad it would be the first time I heard the word "recession," a term it seems I have uttered many more times since.

"You can just do that?" I asked my grandmother, my eyes wide with wonder as we continued our journey to the school. I couldn't believe how hot it was. I had never felt such heat before. I pulled up my white socks and had to skip a little to catch up to my grandmother, who always seemed to walk fast.

It wasn't that we didn't have friendly neighbors back in Brooklyn. There was Willie Mae, whose front door was never locked, facilitating my frequent coming and visiting her daughter, India. India was a couple of years older than me and had recently acquired, much to my fascination, the entire arsenal of hair-care products necessary to maintain her Jheri curl. Willie Mae would give me little chores to do to earn a bit of money — sometimes, I'd rub her aching feet after a night of her tending the bar she owned on Church Avenue. But I had never experienced something like what I shared with my grandmother and those around her. I would later learn that, in those days in Trinidad, it was not unusual for pedestrians to run into a stranger's garage to seek shelter from a passing deluge of rain or for a neighbor to bake a cake for a newly arrived granddaughter from Brooklyn.

Diamond Vale is a suburb designed to house the new and emerging Black middle class. Each street is named after a precious gem — the vale divided into two: the old vale (where my family resided) and the new vale. The two vales were separated by what was once called Diamond Vale Boulevard, a tree-lined street that facilitated cars entering and leaving the neighborhood.

I would continue to be blown away that day. When we arrived at the school on Aquamarine Drive, the principal, Mrs. Spinder, received my grandmother warmly, and they talked like old friends; they weren't, but like in many other conversations my grandmother had, other people's names were rattled off until mutual connections — whether through people or places — could be made. I heard my grandmother tell Mrs. Spinder the story: that I was her granddaughter, that I would be living with her, blah blah blah. I eyed the other kids in the school — they were all of the varying colors of brown and black, like me. Although my school was mainly Black when I had left it back in Brooklyn, I had started at a time when the last vestiges of "White flight" could still be felt. When I started in the second grade, there were four White kids in my class. By the end of the year, there was only one — Naomi. It didn't take long to realize that Naomi was there because her Jewish parents consciously chose to send her there.

At the time, I didn't understand what was happening in Brooklyn. But anyone with eyes could see that there were different worlds divided along racial lines. Mrs. Woodstock, one of the last Whites left in our apartment building on Ocean Avenue, was overly sweet to me and my friends, inviting us into her apartment and offering an abundance of homemade chocolate-chip cookies.

"What are you doing?" her exasperated husband growled over his open newspaper, his irritation with his wife apparent.

"Meet our new neighbors, Stanley!" She genuinely seemed pleased. They left a few months later.

By the time the summer was over and I had started standard five at Diamond Vale Government Primary School, my uncle was in form five at Diego Sec — the secondary school on the boulevard. We both had exams to sit by the end of the school year. As a student in standard five, I had to take the dreaded Common Entrance Exam, an exam that had me working furiously hard to catch up with the other kids in class. Standard five in Trinidad was way above the standard I was used to in Brooklyn. In Brooklyn, we mostly had multiple-choice questions. In standard five, I had to learn a lot of vocabulary words, like "ostentatious," with no multiple choices. Questions had to be answered in essay form, meaning I had to memorize entire pages of text. I would sit for hours in my grandparents' home, at the dining room table, writing and writing whole passages from Shakespeare's *A Midsummer's Night Dream*. I had to perform well to get into a secondary school worth its salt. I had no idea what I was getting myself into — so little that my grandmother asked my teacher to pick my school choices: 1. Holy Name Convent; 2. Providence Girls Catholic School; 3. Woodbrook Secondary School; and 4. Diego Sec, the school right on the boulevard, which my uncle Vince attended.

My uncle had to take his CXC — the Caribbean Examination Council Exams. Modeled heavily after the British school system, students had to pick the subjects they wanted to major in at the end of their second year, with the last three years focused on study, which culminated in exams. The number of subjects you passed significantly impacted your choices as a young adult in Trinidad.

I had already faced a lot of challenges as a child, and although my school life would significantly improve in Trinidad, there was still one major challenge: Mrs. Goddard.

Since I was already close to eleven, I would only be able to sit the exam once. I entered the class of Mrs. Goddard, a red-boned, bow-legged teacher who ruled her class with an iron fist. She took one look at me through her gold-framed glasses. "You too force ripe," she'd say to me, a refrain I will continue to hear from her throughout my tenure under her care. I had never heard that expression before, but I could only imagine her meaning. "You know what it means when a fruit force ripe?" She asked me one day, in front of the entire class. "It's when a fruit looks ripe, but when you bite into it, is sour it sour."

Now, I didn't look ripe.

"Force ripe," a different Goddard repeated the expression to me, once I told her about this encounter, during my trip to Trinidad to bury my grandmother. "What is force ripe? Like a fruit just hanging on a tree, forcing itself to get ripe so somebody will come to pick it?" She sucks her teeth. "This is how we blaming children for the things grown people project onto them. That is violence," she told me.

The classroom that I entered was full of beautiful Black and Brown children. There was the golden-Afroed Colin, who I remember thinking looked so cool. His glasses were strapped tightly on his face with black elastic. There was Dwayne, who seemed to skirt his way around me expertly, and Curtis, whose broad brown face reminded me of the boys I had left back in Brooklyn. My best friend, Joanne Douglas, was there; once she discovered that I lived right around the corner from her, she would pick me up every day. Together we would walk the thirty minutes or so it took to make it up the boulevard to the new vale and school. These walks were instrumental in my learning about this new culture I had landed in. I had already figured out that the games were different: there was no double Dutch and much fewer hand games. I met this new world with wonder — astounded and fascinated by its beauty and simplicity. Everywhere around me were kids and adults who looked like me and sounded like my family. Things seemed so much more relaxed based on the way people walked and talked. It was so beautiful to see Black and Brown people living with so much ease compared to the hustle and bustle of Brooklyn.

In Mrs. Goddard's class, we learned to recite *Song of the Banana Man* by Evan Jones:

Tourism, white man, wiping his face,
Met me in Golden Grove market place.
He looked at m'ol' clothes brown wid stain,
An soaked right through wid de Portland rain,
He has his eye, turn up his nose,

He says, "You're a beggar man, I suppose?"
He says, "Boy, get some occupation,
Be of some value to your nation."
I said, "By God and dis big right han
You mus recognize a banana man."

She would make us do the part of the tourist in a very affected British accent, making us tilt our heads back in an air of arrogance, only to thunder out the words of the Banana man.

"By god and this big left hand, you must recognize a banana man!"

The girls wore plaid overalls and the boys, navy shorts and white shirts. Of course, our sneakers were to be clean and white or you risked getting licks with a wooden ruler on the palm of your open hand.

There's a picture that one of our classmates' fathers took of the class that year. There we are, almost forty kids, some of us, like Alicia, who is now a popular local DJ, staring with a lot of confidence at the camera. In the photo, you can see several students looking behind them and upward. When you read the comments, you understand why: right around that time, while we were being photographed, some child was getting licks from a teacher. Hearing the wails of other children being beaten during school was not out of the norm — getting cuffs, licks. While Mrs. Goddard was a fantastic teacher, and I learned a lot in her classroom, she would never hesitate to box your ear or your back, whip your hand with a wooden ruler or verbally humiliate you in front of the entire class.

The principal, Mrs. Spinder, was wonderful to me. She looked at me and told me that I looked like I could be related to her. She reminded me of Coretta Scott King — because of her hairstyle and dress. Once there was a national agricultural competition, and she picked me to be on her team of students. For a few weeks, we studied plants, mainly in a book — the process of photosynthesis, the different leaves plants can have and how to plant pumpkin, all of which I loved. At the end of the few weeks of harried studying in her office along with two other of my classmates, Mrs. Pinder drove us into the bustling town of Port of Spain, where we would take the exam. She wanted us to win, her brown face open and full of hope. "Allyuh think you can win this?" I can't recall what the prize would have been, but all I wanted was to pass, if only to please this beautiful woman who said that I looked like her family. Unfortunately, we didn't win, but Mrs. Pinder bought us an ice cream afterward and continued to smile warmly at me even long after this experience.

Most mornings, we would commence in the yard, which was the space between three buildings — all the classes would line up, from standard one to standard five, for assembly. Sometimes, if you listened, you would hear us sing:

Jesus wants me for a sunbeam,
A sunbeam, a sunbeam,
I'll be a sunbeam for him.

During these times, you would hear Mrs. Goddard's beautiful voice leading the entire school in song. When Mrs. Goddard sang, it was as though joy was unleashed from her heart and she was transported somewhere where her body relaxed; she smiled even.

Other times, when we had to sing the national anthem, my friends and I would loudly say, "Together we perspire, together we eat cheese," instead of our national motto: "Together we aspire, together we achieve."

The children at Diamond Vale Government Primary were utterly different from those I had left behind in Brooklyn. Back there, most of the kids were well dressed, with clothes that looked newly bought and in style. I had envied my classmates whose parents took them shopping to get them new clothes and school supplies. In Trinidad, we had to wear uniforms, so I didn't have to worry about dressing to impress — not that I ever could. I never tried either. I intuited early that fashion wasn't really about the things you had; it had to do with how you carried them.

In Trinidad, I didn't have to worry about fighting or boys. The boys in my class were not thinking about girls, and the girls were not thinking about boys. It was all about passing the Common Entrance Exam and securing yourself in the best school possible. I felt a huge weight lifted — I could be a kid. I didn't have to fight. And my keen interest in boys thankfully took a back seat to allow me to be a child. So again, catching up academically with the other students in my standard-five class was not even the most complex challenge I had to face; that was learning to acclimate in a way that was... how can I say it? Savory to my standard-five teacher, Mrs. Goddard.

And my arrival did create a stir. "Between your entering our class and Hazel coming to school with her hair out, I knew that that year would be different!" a former classmate recently told me. We both laughed. "I was just watching," he confided. "When you arrived, I just saw that that entire game was about to switch up. And I was right!"

One day, I made the mistake of hanging from the bars in a bus that had come to visit the school. The bus carried a group of twenty-something-year-olds, a film crew. It was the first time I had seen twenty-something-year-olds be artsy. Although I had grown up with my father and his friends, who were all musicians, this group that visited us seemed more hip. I was excited; when we were allowed on the bus, I immediately jumped up on the bars hanging from the ceiling and swung around a bit. I remember feeling good — exhilarated even. The other students started laughing, looking at me, their faces full of awe. I loved it. I had a great time; it wasn't long before some other kids joined me. Again, we laughed, hanging and swinging from the bars. It felt so liberating. I was out of breath by the time we returned to the classroom, so much fun had I had.

Mrs. Goddard was furious. Her usually stern face was even more severe, and she held her wooden ruler, the one she would whack us on the palms with, dangerously in her hand. "Allyuh acting like you don't know how to behave yourselves. Climbing on the bus like a bunch of monkeys. Who started it?" *How did she even know?* I remember thinking — she wasn't even there! I immediately began to sink in my seat. But she knew. "Ms. Force Ripe, is you. Don't think I don't know. Come here," she demanded as she stood at the front of the classroom, her arms behind her back and the dreaded wooden ruler in one hand. I walked up front, my head hung low, past the wooden desks that opened from the top.

"Turn around!" she demanded. I had no idea what she was going to do. A feeling of dread grabbed me; I felt my insides recoil in terror. As soon as she turned around, she demanded, "Put your hands up!" She then began to whack my calves furiously, seemingly with all the power in her body. I had marks on my calves for weeks. I cried and cried. I couldn't wait to go home and tell my grandmother. I knew once I told her what Mrs. Goddard had done to me, she'd let me quit school. When I was even younger, I had attended a small school up the street from my grandparent's house. One day the teacher made me cry, and when I went home and told my grandmother, she told me I didn't have to go back. I knew for sure she would be on my side. That she would protect me like she always had done.

I was crushed by the time I got home. I would become even more crushed when my grandmother told me I had to return to school.

As cruel as I may have thought Mrs. Goddard to be, I know her heart was in the right place. A former classmate from this class said, "Yes, there was corporal punishment. That was the system. And some teachers had malice in their hearts; you could see it. But Mrs. Goddard? If she recognized you had talent, she would ensure you did something with that talent."

In Trinidad and Tobago, beating children in school is no longer legal. However, it is still within the rights of parents to do so. Our legacy of beating our children is a colonial one. There are dozens of historical observations (if not more) of Indigenous people being astounded by the Europeans' brutality toward their children. On my trip back to Trinidad to bury my grandmother, I would meet and talk to activist Gillian Goddard. She shared with me that she chose to homeschool her children rather than send them into what she sees as a school system that still practices colonial violence. She talked about how adults, in general, are abusive to children, and when several schools decided to demonstrate against climate change during my visit, her face opened up wide with happiness, full of hope for our future.

5.

One woman's progress

In his *Guardian* article of 5 April 2021, "Bill Gates is the biggest private owner of farmland in the United States," writer Nick Estes reminds us of the relationship between land, power, race and class, as well as how we have come to relate to land — and often the answer to the question of who owns, labors and cares for it reveals "obscene levels of inequality and legacies of colonialism and white supremacy in the United States, and also the world." Estes argues that "wealth accumulation always goes hand-in-hand with exploitation and dispossession."

Frantz Fanon reminds us that "for a colonized people the most essential value, because the most concrete, is first and foremost the land: the land which will bring them bread and, above all, dignity."

I've never really understood the concept of privately owned land. When I read stories about how many Indigenous people were confused about settlers' use and control of land, I always understood it from their point of view. It seems silly that anyone can say they "own" a piece of land. The land, to me, should be shared; taken care of, yes, but never owned. I think ownership is a faulty foundation that only encourages violence toward the land and her people. To claim land ownership means one must protect it and acquire more. This is the foundation of Europeans' many wars, which they believed are their biblical right. The history of land ownership is a bloody one, which perhaps helps us to understand why "terror" and "terra" phonetically sound not so unalike.

Like most of their generation, my grandparents were raised in rural communities. My grandfather was born in the Indo-Trinidadian heartland of Caroni and my grandmother in the mountain village of Santa Cruz. My grandparents came of age over the course of two world wars on an island that was considered valuable to foreign interests even before the discovery of oil there.

My grandfather, a *dougla* (half East Indian, half Black), raised by what my grandmother would call a creole family — creole in this sense meaning Black Trinidadian — had the word "coolie" written on his birth certificate. He was rendered an orphan when his parents migrated to Canada — his mother would die from the "draft"— a word that, for Black people, came to mean both the cold air of temperate regions as well as the racism typically experienced in these spaces; his father, who was originally from Guyana, was never to be heard from again.

My grandparents' house is painted turquoise. While most of the other places in our neighborhood have been renovated — extensions added, floors added, fancy facades added — ours is pretty much the same one-story concrete home that was built initially. We all grew up hearing that the house was bought from Eric Williams's daughter. I remember the day my grandmother came breathlessly into the house, the sweat from the hot sun dotting her face. I was rocking on the wicker chair, my bare feet enjoying the smoothness of the newly polished granite floor.

"I just paid the house off," she told me, slumping down in the lazy brown-leather chair. But, of course, I was just a child and didn't appreciate the accomplishment inherent in such a statement.

The house is not fancy. There is no hot water. There is a small living room when you enter, followed by a kitchen and passageway that leads to three small bedrooms. There is a washroom outside the kitchen door, with a large sink and washing board. The house looks pretty much the same as when I left. There are still the pictures of Pope John Paul II (my grandmother's favorite), the Queen of England and a very Europeanized Jesus and Mary.

Punctuating these cultural interlopers are photos of different family members — every grandchild's appearance suggesting the various backgrounds that our lineage reflects. There are the lighter ones, referred to as "red," and the browner ones, ranging from earthy textures to the deep brown of tamarind seeds. There are the ones with hair that recalls India, those with hair that reflects Africa and those with hair that connects the two and the land we're on. We are Trinidad and Tobago in all of her historical ramifications.

It is said that my grandmother wanted to buy this house and that my grandfather, always erring on the side of humility, was against leaving the wood house he had built with his own hands in the valley of Santa Cruz. He didn't want to move into what could only be described as a mimicry of US suburbia. There must be advantages to living in a wood house in the Caribbean. I'm not sure about the usefulness of concrete.

6.

The burial

It's the day of my grandmother's funeral. The night before, my uncle Vince and I sat at the side of the house. A pandemonium of parrots made its daily flight above our heads, over the hills, away from the setting sun. Later on in this trip, when I'm walking in the botanical gardens with Gillian Goddard, she will tell me about the British man who came out with a pellet gun to shoot them every evening. "He thought they were too noisy. He hated them."

"Haven't you cried yet?" I asked my uncle between my tears. Throughout the day, I'd be reminded of my grandmother and start to cry. It could be something as simple as picking up a cup and remembering the day I sat with her in a diner and she rolled it up in paper towels; and now, here it was. I love that about my grandmother. I love that there is a part of her that is subversive.

Together my uncle and I finished a bottle of vodka. "Who, me? Cry?" my uncle responded. "Crying is just about us. Hildred never needed us. But we needed her." I began to cry again. He laughed.

"Whathappentoyou?" He sucked his teeth, pulled at his earlobe and laughed. I laughed too. When he's not talking about religion, he's still the Vince you'd walk up to Covigne with to buy weed from the Rastas or who insisted that the usually quiet street of Emerald Drive hear the wailings of Ozzy Osbourne. This is the visit that makes me realize what a loss I had experienced when I left Trinidad, and that one of the greatest losses was the friendship of my uncle Vince. "This place wasn't the same after you left," he'd tell me one day as we're driving to Blanchisseuse, "the house was so quiet." I never thought about the space that I had left, what it was like without me.

On the day of my grandmother's funeral, I awake with a splitting headache. I must stink of alcohol. But I don't care. I am distraught. My hair is an unkempt mess, a cardinal sin in this community. My clothes are not ironed, which, too, is a cardinal sin. My discomfort continues on the drive to Santa Cruz, with its high altitude and curvy mountainside roads that leave me on the verge of nausea. In fact, during the actual funeral, I will have to excuse myself to perhaps vomit in the lavatory.

I had imagined that the service would be delivered by a priest who knew her — my entire life, my grandmother was closely associated with whatever parish she found herself in. Growing up, she was always talking about Father this or Father that. She was a part of the Catholic community, waking up early in the morning to bake bread for priests (much to my grandfather's chagrin) and hold prayer vigils with others in the community to ensure the protection of children or that coming bills could be paid. But the priest who presided over her funeral — despite our being in the very church in which she had been christened as a baby, confirmed and married — seemed bored, distant, not at all connected to who my grandmother was, not at all concerned about her connection to the village we had all now found ourselves in.

I can barely deliver the words my family asked me to write. One of my childhood best friends comes to the pulpit and places her hand on my back. I look out at a sea of faces who are all gathered to celebrate my grandmother's life. My hair is wild; I am wearing jeans and an oversized black blouse. I am wearing black sneakers. Again, I did not iron my clothes. My grief is great. Everything is just a blur. But I console myself that at least after the funeral the family will all gather at my grandparents' home, console one another and laugh at the old times, conjure stories of Mammy and Grandaddy and hold each other in our grief, gather around it, become closer because of it. It is what my grandmother would have wanted.

In my eulogy, I talk about the fact that she and my grandfather had been married for fifty years and that she had survived him by twenty-five. My mother would later tell me that on the night following her funeral, my grandfather had visited her and said, "Finally! I've been waiting all these years."

7.

Dotish tour

Moving to Trinidad was an exciting and enriching experience. While Brooklyn was fast, new and big, Trinidad was much slower, older (but in a good way) and smaller. While I jumped double Dutch in Brooklyn, I played hopscotch on the pavement in front of my grandparents' house. I learned to adjust because I had to — as much as possible. By the time I was around twelve, the only two things that interested me were books and boys.

The summer after I started in form two at Providence, my uncle took me to all the pubs and parties he could. Although I was way under age, we usually managed to stay, buy drinks and smoke cigarettes, which was the extent of our mischief. I never had anything bad happen to me. We all felt safe. We never worried about anything. When we had no car, we'd hitch rides into town or to the mall.

I got into Providence Girls Catholic School, located in Belmont, an old neighborhood home to many artists. At one point, a community of formerly enslaved people from America had lived there, and in any case, it was a neighborhood full of history. The school was atop a hill, and if you didn't have a car, like me, you'd have to take a taxi to Port of Spain, Independence Square, and then take a maxi taxi (which is cheaper than a taxi) back to Belmont. If you had a car or a ride, you'd have to drive around the savannah, and the street was right off of it, after the road to Maraval. Or you'd have to walk, which I often did. Luckily for me, however, I often got a lift with my friend Ashby from my standard-five class, who had also gotten into Providence. So, many mornings, her family would squeeze me in for the ride from Diamond Vale to Belmont. I love this family: they are beautiful, Black, intelligent and kind. I loved riding with them, admiring their caring dynamics and feeling their love.

The uniform was similar to St. Joseph's Convent, Providence's sister school, except our turquoise polyester skirt was sewn with three pleats and our white blouses buttoned from the back with circular collars. On the first day of school, we were met by a prefect (I didn't know what the word meant until then) who exuded an older-girl cool I hoped to capture one day. Her uniform hugged her curvy body, whereas mine was bought too big so I would grow into it and not have to buy another (it was to last me five years).

I was excited to be in secondary school! I was excited to be at Providence! The other students starting with me were myriad shades and colors. Although we were all in uniform, the hairstyles were different and reflected the times — the Eighties — and big hair, no matter the texture, was all the rage. But most of the girls were, like me, still in that awkward stage, and many had hair still in childish hairstyles. I suddenly felt a relief I had never felt in my entire life: I was surrounded only by other girls. I felt relaxed by this. It didn't take me long to realize that I loved attending an all-girls school. All the form-one girls looked awkward like me.

Like most, if not all, former colonies of European countries, Trinidad and Tobago had never really been allowed to develop a vision of itself outside of European imperialist structures. Like every other colonial region globally, the West was indeed there, ensuring that the poor would continue to be exploited and excluded through economic policies or use of the military. While we have always had a Black or Brown prime minister since being "given" independence from "Great" Britain, our political, economic, educational and to some extent our cultural systems could be understood through Frantz Fanon's *Black Skin, White Masks*. Published in 1952 in France, this work is one of the first to look at the pathological impact of colonization on the colonized. He realized that colonization fosters mental disturbance, cognitive dissonance, double consciousness. Colonization prevents an independent sense of identity and this negatively impacts psychological development. As colonized subjects are taught white is positive and human, while Black is evil, subhuman and so not viable, the Black person will therefore grow up and negate their own Blackness to aspire to Whiteness. This process has individual and collective consequences. This is why, when I attempt to enter the country of my foremothers, it is a woman who looks like me who metes out the most border violence I have yet experienced. I imagine even though she looks like me, she feels compelled to treat me with such little regard. This is how we internalize oppression.

But still, many things in our culture came not from our colonial masters but were handed down gently, with love, from our African, East Indian and Indigenous ancestors. Sometimes this looks like a Yoruba feast in the village of Gasparilla. I will be taken there by Robert Young — a Trinidadian artist and founder of the Cloth, a pan-Caribbean clothing line — in his Jeep along with two others: his assistant Michelle, a White British woman, and Sage, a beautiful, gay East Indian man who will tell me on more than one occasion about the importance of taking care of one's yard. It will not be till much later in the evening that I would realize I was on one of Young's "dotish tours" — "dotish" in Trinbagonian means stupid.

At this feast, the villagers gather, and I hear a chorus of drumming that puts me in a trance as I witness hierarchy turned on its head. For it is here that the people take back their power. Here, as an American, you are nothing. You are nothing because you do not know these drums, so you must listen. You are nothing because you do not know the songs sung, although they sound familiar, along with the rhythms conjured by drums. But this nothingness is beautiful. It is here, in this space, where every age is represented — from babies to great-grandmothers — in the darkness of the early morning, that I find a connection to another dimension, back to another continent that has always provided the world with its heartbeat and, so, its rhythm.

8.

Sweet, sweet
T&T

We are the daughters of lost nations
Born to parents of forced migrations.

Coming of age on alien land,
Speaking in tongues few understand.

We are the daughters of lands torn asunder —
of lands left to rot, by colonial masters.

Erased are the lineages, needed for survival,
Wisdom replaced with lies and their bibles.

The texts of our lives are written in blood,
Spilled on the earth, seeped into mud.

With hands full of love,
We must fashion from this.
Mold it to life
With our very own breaths.

Breaths that are ancient
Breaths from the depth,
Breaths from the living
& breaths from the dead.

Breaths that are healing,
& breaths that give birth
Breaths that are sacred

As life-giving Earth.

We would say "Current gone" when the electricity stopped, which it often did. "Watah gone!" when WASA, the local waterworks, did the same. It was cozy. It forced us to come together and figure out solutions. If watah gone, I'd have to go next door to my aunt's to shower, which I didn't mind, because they had a water heater. When the electricity was gone, we'd have to light candles. The storyteller in my aunt would reveal herself: she'd tell us about la Diablesse and Soucouyant — the former so vain she made a deal with the devil: her soul for eternal beauty. She has a cow foot you cannot see under her long, beautiful dress, and she lures men into the forest with her beauty. Soucouyant appears as a ball of light, a woman who sucks you dry. While captivated by my aunt's storytelling, I didn't want to hear horror stories about loose women. I was starving for stories of brave girls and women who were in control of their own lives.

As fate would have it, I was able to travel to Trinidad a second time that same year. This time I flew through Houston and discovered that my money was rendered useless by cashless payments, and that there were also Trinis in Texas. Rookman, an octogenarian from Couva, sat next to me and pulled out a book, which she carefully placed on my lap. *Health in Your Hands* by Devandra Vora is a book about acupressure therapy (reflexology). I drank up her words, in which I could hear my late grandmother's voice, and settled into the flight that would take me again to Trinidad. During this trip, I had the privilege of reading at the Bocas Lit Festival and meeting many other Caribbean writers and poets. There were poetry slams, readings, workshops and literary stars such as Margaret Busby, Britain's youngest and first Black woman publisher. I heard the Trinbagonian writer Barbara Johnson read, and met other Trinbagonian writers such as Attilah Springer, Soyini Nneka and Andre Bagoo. There were books on sale and various artisanal products, and even Gillian, through the organization she co-founded called Chocolate Rebellion, had a table full of locally made chocolate products, offering a "post-colonial chocolate tasting." There were tasty, locally made dried fruits such as bananas and watermelon, along with information about their Port of Spain chocolate tours.

While there, I met a photographer, a young Indian man, who rushed out of the venue at the National Library and Information System (NALIS), telling me as he hung up his cell phone, "I have to go, you know how many murders we have last night?" On this trip, I stayed in an apartment not too far from the savannah with wooden floors, and took walks at the botanical gardens with Gillian Goddard, where I saw blooming poui trees.

I slept in a bedroom that had a brood of nesting parrots in the ceiling, and every week I had a box of local organic fruits and vegetables delivered courtesy of the New Rural Alliance, a cooperative that Goddard and a host of other local farmers began to support the local organic farming community. In the boxes, in which no plastic was used, would be plantains, star fruit, coconuts, pineapples and other fruits and vegetables that reminded me of my grandmother. I also took walks along the savannah, that great expanse of green that could, in a way, be likened to the heart of Port of Spain, that place that we flock to for sports, family outings and Carnival. Most evenings, if I remembered, I could see the setting sun outside the living room apartment.

As I am not a citizen of Trinidad and Tobago, I am only allowed to stay a maximum of three months, so I left with much sadness, vowing to return. By this time, I had figured that it made sense for me to continue the process of learning about the land of my ancestors. Despite being born to Trinidadian parents, and even having lived in Trinidad, there was still so much for me to learn. After meeting Gillian, I felt I had been given a teacher, and if I was willing, I could become a student. With this in mind, I thought of returning to Trinidad. I wanted to go through the cycle of planting seeds to experience cultivation and harvest. I wanted to spend more time in this landscape, to get to know the many other forms of life there: the iguana and the leatherback turtles who lay their eggs in Toco each year. I wanted to learn more about the mountains and the bush. And Gillian Goddard promised to be a most capable teacher.

Part Three

1.

Hindsight is 20/20
March 2020

New York is the last place I'd want to be in the face of a global collapse. But as fate would have it, it's precisely where I found myself as the novel coronavirus, Covid-19, became a global pandemic. Surely there'd be the chaos of panic-buying and lawlessness. But that didn't happen. It turned out that the scariest thing is the news. Before the pandemic, the news peddled stories like that of a Dallas dancer whose fall off a thirteen-foot pole is shown over and over again — the disturbing plummet, her landing face first, her body splayed briefly like a lifeless ragdoll, her subsequent jerking, shocked response in twerks — on every news channel and talk show across the country. She suffered a broken jaw, cracked teeth and a sprained ankle. The scene attracted over six million views. I couldn't watch the video more than once — I grew sad that no one was commenting on the fact that, in all of her vulnerability — financial and otherwise — this young woman's life was put in danger to "earn" a living.

The never-ending barf of sophisticated trash emitted from American television never ceases to amaze me. Most times, I am successful at not watching, but with my mother, the television sits omnipresent, always turned on, upon the throne of her dressing table. There's the obscene number of pharmaceuticals peddled on the screen, along with their dire side effects. Then there's our pinnacle of cultural achievement: the reality show. Everything we do and make as Americans — from our commercials to our programming, our fashion to our culture — is a product. We assault the world's consciousness and intelligence with our media, our fast culture, our ways of consuming and our lifestyle. We are the pinnacle of crass consumerism. We are that shining example: for us, freedom has always meant the opportunity to consume, based on markets of debt/death. I loathe it. But I am also deeply fascinated by it.

And now I was at its mercy as the pandemic hit, and thankfully, as if a gift from the gods, there was something that my mother and I could do together, and that was watch *90-Day Fiancé* and its franchise offshoots. Chronicling the exploits of citizens of this settler state on their journey to finding "real" love and cashing in on America's hunger for reality programming, *90-Day Fiancé* chronicles couples as they traverse the K-1 visa process. This is a visa given to a non-US citizen engaged to a US citizen, and tens of thousands are granted annually. The idea is that the non-citizens can travel to the US and, in ninety days, either marry (and so begin becoming a legal resident and citizen), return home or risk deportation.

Except what's revealed is deeply disturbing: There's Angela, a White fifty-something-year-old woman from Texas who's engaged to Michael, a twenty-three-year-old, baby-faced Nigerian. Angela is very abusive to her much younger fiancé. Then there's Ed, the stereotypically overconfident American White guy — who we first meet flying out to the Philippines to meet his fiancé, twenty-three-year-old Rosemary Vega. The latter seems so young you wonder if she's of legal age. In the end, the series exposes the insanity that gets rolled up into ideas of "love" in the field of green cards, empire, borders and sex.

It's interesting to watch couples navigate this process, and I often wonder what the show says about us as Americans. Many of the people on the show seem clueless and insensitive to different cultures — when Ed visits his much younger Filipina girlfriend in the Philippines, his discomfort about staying in her modest home is palpable. In one scene, she attempts to help him at a market, and he accuses her of trying to rip him off, so great is his paranoia that he is being used for a green card. Another couple is composed of a much older American woman from Ohio (Babygirl Lisa) who falls in love with a Nigerian, much younger boyfriend, Usman. She is fifty and not very attractive, but she has the kind of confidence only a mediocre White woman who knows the power of Whiteness can have. To be fair, though, Usman is no victim here. He's a pop star and utilizes all the publicity he can get to promote himself. *90-Day Fiancé* reveals, among other things, how inequities embedded in our systems of immigration can promote exploitative and abusive behavior. It's a reality show on steroids, a mirror that reflects the distorted values that emerge in narcissistic cultures.

2.

Turtle Island

When I first left Copenhagen, I had a stopover in London, where I stayed overnight at Yotel, a capsule hotel where a room, or pod, is ten square meters. I find it cozy; it is replete with cable and a shower. Although there is not one plant to be seen, the room does its job of ensuring me a good night's rest. Before bed, I walk around the airport, where I score a dahl dinner. While waiting in line to pay for my meal, I study the mountains of food at Marks & Spencer's. Unlike in my bank account, abundance is all around me, available only to those who can pay. Seemingly everything you could ever need is here: from avocados to hairbrushes. I wonder about all the food on display: the perfectly shaped bell peppers, the apples red and shiny. Later, when I am in Trinidad, I will notice that the fruit and vegetables there are more rugged and natural-looking. I know that there is no way that all of this food gets bought.

When I arrived in Trinidad as a child, my grandmother took my spiritual growth seriously. Although I was already ten, I still had not had my first communion. Living in my grandmother's home meant attending mass weekly, getting my first communion and being confirmed. I enjoyed attending church — for the social as much as the spiritual aspects. While most stories in the bible were neither here nor there for me, I always did like the story of Jesus in the temple. I've always loved the anti-capitalist vibe of that story. And this is the story that comes back to me in London as I think of how these shops and malls have become our modern-day places of worship. I smile as I picture myself comically kicking down the pyramids of food, smashing things to the ground, declaring, "This is madness!" Yet, here in this shopping center, our human weaknesses are laid bare: the conflation of culture with consumerism; the illusion of an abundance of things that come from far away; the lack of fresh air; the plasticity of it all; the lack of plants in my Yotel — what was this future we seemed to be hurrying toward so quickly?

When I arrive at Turtle Island, Bolsonaro's Brazil means that the Amazon is burning in Abya Yala. His party hastens its demise; before his leadership, it had been on the mend. These forests are considered the world's lungs: What can we do without them? As mentioned before, the lungs are where we hold our grief, and I understand why the earth is grieving. Abya Yala provides the Global North with wood from its felled trees for its "sustainable" fuel, and soy for its animals whose deaths are profit.

The rains that arrive with me have re-awakened our splendid plant relations. The damp streets teem with flourishing plant life. Between the petrichor and blooming tropical foliage that abounds in Southern California, I feel held by nature despite the concrete around me. Unlike the people of this planet, these plants can migrate freely, so they are found growing throughout this region. I am in awe of the birds of paradise that also abound in Trinbagonian gardens. The huge aloe vera and agave plants in the gardens dwarf any I left back in my apartment in Copenhagen.

When I walk through the streets of Echo Park, the humidity and lushness make me feel connected to Abya Yala in a way that I don't think about on the East Coast. There's something about the fact that the land runs all along the south, center and north to Kalaallit Nunaat (Greenland) that I feel in my blood. I remember the day I realized I could trace my finger from the southernmost point of Abya Yala and run it up to Greenland. "Look at this," I showed Aka, the Inuit poet and activist, one day when she was visiting me in Copenhagen. "Our ancestors must have hung out," and we laughed at this.

When I arrived, the united settler nation state of America — a nation founded on land theft and genocide — declared itself to be "having a migrant crisis." This declaration lays its beliefs and character bare. Before the arrival of Europe's excesses, we traveled freely along the paths I traced with my finger that day in Copenhagen. Borders are a tool of genocide. The fact that I could technically walk back to the country of my mother's birth from here is comforting.

There are continued reports of "unaccompanied minors" and mass graves at the border. Anything that limits the movement of people will inevitably kill. Children are separated from their parents — these children will go on to spend years at detention facilities where they are sometimes farmed out to American families under the institution of "foster care" — a system that is rooted in Eurocentric fundamentalism and whose legacies can be seen in the tragedy of residential schools, and by extension in how the entire Western genocidal system has come to express itself, including in its epidemic of mass shootings. Some of these children will perish in these death camps, some of these children will disappear.

Echo Park, the neighborhood where I will stay for about a week, has all the signs of displacement and settlement: hip coffee shops amid shuttered buildings and the epidemic of houselessness that has descended upon this nation, especially after the financial crisis of 2008. It is the place where artists such as a young Ishmael Reed wrote his second novel *Yellow*

Back Radio Broke-Down during the Sixties as the country exploded in racial reckonings. It was also the place where the silent movie era was launched. Echo Park has a strong artist and political history, and is considered the epicenter of LA's gentrification battle. Later on in this trip, I will read Isabel Wilkerson's *Caste: The Origins of Our Discontent*, in which she draws parallels between three systems of apartheid that have existed or continues to exist: that of Blacks in America, of the Dalit in India's caste system, and of the Third Reich. It is a bold and necessary comparison, its limits forgiven in light of the bridge that connects across oceans, people and oppressions. For Wilkerson, "America is an old house. We can never declare the work over" — a house which demands care and attention. "Choose not to look, however, at your own peril." Like any house, the foundation must be tended to. "Unaddressed, the ruptures and diagonal cracks will not fix themselves." And like an old house, "America has an unseen skeleton, a caste system…" For Wilkerson, caste and race can coexist, but are not synonymous or mutually exclusive. "Cast is the bones, race the skin."

Casteism and racism often occurs at simultaneously — the former "is about positioning and restricting those positions, vis-à-vis others… race and racism… confuse and distract from the underlying structural and more powerful Sith Lord of caste. Like the cast of a broken arm, like the cast in a play, a caste system holds everyone in a fixed place." Wilkerson also talks about the "narcissistic nation," and I wonder what this image of itself is that the united settler states of America is so in love with that it cannot wrestle itself from its own reflection and attend to its humanity.

Kaiama L. Glover offers a look into narcissism, in *A Regarded Self: Caribbean Womanhood and the Ethics of Disorderly Being*. She does this through the lens of Caribbean female characters through literature by authors such as Maryse Conde, among others. Examining how certain characters "disorder their narrative communities" through the "regarded self", which is a term Glover borrows from Nigerian visual artist and photographer Ike Ude and captures the ambivalence of being a "social being, wherein it is at once crucial to love oneself, deeply and protectively, and to publicly perform modesty, selflessness and love for one's community." For the author, there is a continuum of self-regard and she highlights each character's behaviors "ranging from self-concern to selfishness, from selfcare to something brazenly akin to narcissism." Glover admits that "narcissism" is a big word and gives us a bit of history on it: that it was first coined by Sigmund Freud "as a normal psychological condition constitutive of the fundamental human drive to defend the integrity of self, narcissism so defined amounts to a "libidinal complement to the egoism of the instinct of self-preservation." Narcissism, she says, "is perceived as a distinctly North Atlantic pathology, the inevitable product of a coldly individualistic culture." Narcissism of the pathological nature, she writes, arises like all other pathologies, as a coping mechanism. "It is an individual's means of contending with her or his perceived vulnerability to the psychosocial assaults of the outside world and, as such, can be a far more nuanced term than popular understandings would have us believe." She cites psychoanalyst Heinz Kohut and his 1966 essay "Forms and Transformations of Narcissism." For Kohut, narcissism is "a necessary adaptive strategy, a survivalist impulse to provide resources for the self in moments or spaces wherein that self is denied sustenance — or denied altogether." It is in this nonpathological way that the author wants us to regard narcissism. She reminds us that Frantz Fanon takes up the subject of narcissism, "albeit ambivalently" as a "defensive response to one's community and its order..." in his *Black Skin, White Masks*. "On one hand," the author notes, "Fanon condemns narcissism as an essentialist obstacle to his idea of race-blind human solidarity. Yet, on the other, he hints at the possibility of a dynamically narcissistic practice of individual disalienation whereby it becomes possible to refuse the psychic violation of hostile external forces." In other words, narcissism could also be viewed as a praxis of extreme self-consciousness and was a sort of "escape valve." It's a fascinating analysis on narcissism, a subject that has received much traction since the election of Trump, and one I would encourage you to look into with more depth.

LA is the first stop on my book tour, which includes San Francisco, Portland, New York, Baltimore, St. Paul, Minneapolis, Helsinki and Turku (Finland) and Trondheim (Norway), among other cities both in the US and outside it. I'm invited to Johns Hopkins by scholar Robbie Shilliam. While there, we take a walk on campus. He tells me about Baltimore's unique history as a border town: it sits right on the Mason-Dixon line, and northbound trains once desegregated while southbound trains segregated at this stop.

My friend and former Flux roommate Jason Smalls meets me at LAX airport. He's a slender, deep-brown brother who is also one of the most intelligent people I know. As mentioned, it's the height of the "border crisis" in the US, and headlines declare, "Kids in cages." My sister friend Kelly Curry has gone to the US/Mexican border more than once to assist the humans who find themselves, like their ancestors, under the regime of Eurocentric fundamentalist borders. Like other borders on the rest of Turtle Island, including Abya Yala, this border was created by White settlers through invasion and war.

The story dominates the news. Although Jason had grown up in LA, he has never been to the Mexican border. Neither have I, so we drive there to see what's happening. Jason's parents migrated to Los Angeles like so many others from the South (as documented in the many stories in another work of Isabella Wilkerson's, *The Warmth of Other Suns*), seeking better opportunities, only to find, as publishing veteran Marie D. Brown once said, LA "is the south."

Sitting in a small Airbnb kitchen, I ask him what it was like to grow up in LA in the Eighties. When I left Brooklyn in the early Eighties, I had ensured I missed the beginning of the crack epidemic.

"Well, I lived in the hood in the Eighties," he tells me, emptying the contents of a cigar onto the small kitchen table. He's got a Cheshire-cat grin and long thin dreads that fall over his face. Although he's the same age as me, inching close to fifty, he still maintains his lithe skater body. "All the kids say I look like Travis Scott," he says to me, grinning.

"Who's Travis Scott?" I ask, and he laughs.

***

"So, was it *Boyz n the Hood* dangerous?" I ask once we're in his svelte ride and buckled in. I don't drive and have never had a genuine interest in cars. But I can appreciate a nice car — and his car is excellent.

"Yeah, but there hasn't been an urban LA movie — I guess *Menace II Society* would be the closest representation. But, unfortunately, no one ever did it justice because it was way more dangerous than *Menace*."

"Word?!"

"Look," he says, flashing me that expression he always gives when he's about to break something down, "no matter how many official denials you hear, you know that the government was involved. Urban inner-city, at least Los Angeles, the late Seventies, early Eighties — you had Russian-produced military-grade assault rifles in the hands of fourteen-year-olds who had never been outside their communities, let alone the country." He expertly pulls out of his parking space and we hit the road. "They didn't have the contacts to meet people with Russian-grade military weapons. So you've got the hood, a recession, Colombian cocaine and Russian-made assault rifles. And that's a crazy mix." He laughs, flashing his wide smile.

When Ronald Reagan became president in 1981, he attacked not only unions but poor Black communities as well. Declaring a "war" on drugs, Reagan put his vice president, George H.W. Bush, a former CIA director, in charge. Congressional committee figures revealed that before Bush's appointment, thirty-four tons of cocaine were coming into the country annually, but that after he was appointed the "anti-drug czar," that figure went up to eighty-five tons of cocaine. The Iran/Contra scandal exposed the fact that, when the US Congress cut off funds to right-wing Contras in Nicaragua, the US government raised money by secretly selling arms to Iran and importing drugs it smuggled from Nicaragua to sell to local, mostly Black drug dealers in San Francisco and LA, which primarily ended up further destroying impoverished communities and barrios of Southern California. This played a significant role in destabilizing North and Central America, giving birth to the conditions many people attempt to flee from today. Senator John Kerry's chief subcommittee investigator,

Jack Blum, has admitted that, while the CIA did not directly have agents selling drugs to fund the Contras, "the United States government may have opened up channels that helped drug dealers bring drugs into the United States and protected them from law enforcement."

In the groundbreaking book *We Charge Genocide: The Historic Petition to the United Nations for Relief From a Crime of the United States Government Against the Negro People*, we are reminded that "the war on drugs was an act of governmental genocide. Millions of young lives were damaged or snuffed out completely. Families were destroyed, and whole communities were turned into drug war zones and left to rot away by the government on all levels. Tens of thousands went to prison. This was a conscious government policy with the main target being African Americans and other working people of color. We Charge Genocide!"

Months later, when I'm in Oakland, I will learn from the transactivist Ira X that, prior to this flooding of weapons and drugs into Los Angeles, the inhabitants of South Central had organized themselves so that they did not have to engage with the police. X's father, George Edward Armstrong, was a local burglar before becoming politicized by the Black Panther Party. Both of X's parents were heavily invested in the Rainbow Coalition, which was based on Chairman Fred Hampton's belief in organizing across racial lines. Many believe that this is why he was murdered, at the young age of twenty-three, while he lay sleeping next to his pregnant wife in Chicago, Ira X says. The Panthers had recognized that once people were housed, could provide for themselves and their families, crime went down. They had a framework around livelihood. Organized as a neighborhood watch, folks began to rely on each other in a way that discouraged police intervention. They began to govern themselves. What good was calling the police, anyway? They had realized that the presence of the police could mean getting brutalized, raped, having your things stolen, being framed, deported or even shot.

Ira X tells me that, in 1983, the three cities where drugs and arms were brought in were all Black Panther hotspots: Oakland, Los Angeles and Chicago. "This really created a situation where the police were coming back into neighborhoods."

We're driving through South Central on the freeway, heading south through what Jason calls "the hood." I lament the streets lined, seemingly forever, by tents and people rendered houseless by the callousness of our monetary system, which in the end is based on thin air.

"You know what someone said to me the other day when we were talking about poverty?" Kelly once asked me. When I shook my head "no," she continued: "The best way to help the poor is not to become one." Kelly laughed. "Ain't that some shit?"

3.

Borderlands

Isabel Wilkerson's *Caste* equips me with a better lens through which to see America. Of course, there are fundamental differences between India's caste system, Nazi Germany and the racist hierarchical system we live under. Still, I find the comparisons and contrasts helpful for mining some understanding of what is happening in the US. It seems that, with every trip I take, the racial and wealth divide becomes deeper and deeper: poor folks are displaced, wealthier people settle in formerly underserved communities, the demarcation almost always racial — as in Echo Park.

"Man, the US needs to get its priorities straight," I groan as Jason and I continue to drive past tents on LA's notorious Skid Row, which now runs over fifty city blocks. Skid Row has been in existence since the 1930s, but I doubt anyone could have predicted how large it has become. With some numbers suggesting up to 15,000 stable residents, it is one of the largest settlements of houseless people in the nation. It resembles some kind of post-Apocalyptic scene. There is no way to travel here and escape the fact that this country is in a deep crisis — between opioid addiction, houselessness, mass incarceration, impoverishment, mass shootings, the healthcare crisis and economic instability. And this was before the pandemic. So many of those living in tents fought in wars waged in faraway lands, not realizing that when they came back, their experiences would too.

"Yeah, well, the US isn't that bad," he countered as I cocked my eyebrow challengingly at him.

"Look," he wound his car window down. "Fuck Trump!" he yelled out into the air. He did this at least three more times while we were on the road, the Pacific Ocean caressing our journey. "See!" He looked over at me with triumph on his beautiful face.

"See what?"

"Well, if America was evil…" he said while flashing his wide smile, "we'd get into so much trouble." And as if to underscore his point, he stuck his head out the window and yelled one more time for good measure, "Fuck Trump!"

On our way to the border, we stop in Carlsbad. We enter a shopping mall where the workers are the only other people of color. I put my scarf over my head, knowing it will make us stand out even more. But instead, Jason flashes his broad smile: "Oh, I see what you're doing." And we laugh our way back to the car, past confused stares, happy because we're on the road, that journey which is the quintessential American adventure, indoctrinated in us by movies and the car industry.

We park the car not too far from the border in San Diego and walk across the bridge to Mexico. As we drove toward the border, there was a stark difference between the manicured landscape of San Diego and the concentration of housing on the other side. There's a Mennonite family being detained — as they are not allowed to have any picture identification. When we enter Mexico, there's the color, the chaotic energy of people meeting at various points of arrival and departure. There are bars, restaurants and mariachi singers, and all along the streets when you first enter Mexico are camps of people — primarily brown — who have made the arduous journey to a place they hope can offer some safety, some comfort — where the same government that perhaps destabilized their own now seems to be the only savior. I note that they look just like me. They are of the same earthy brown complexion as I am, their hair just like mine. They could have been my family, I remember thinking, and realizing that these people the media are talking about, are basically my relatives.

4.

Colonialism 2.0

On the second day of my arrival, Kelly drives up from the border to meet me. Like during the "migrant crisis" in Europe just five years before, these migrants from the Northern Triangle of Central America — El Salvador, Guatemala, and Honduras — are fleeing violence, whether that of gangs, poverty or government regimes that are probably financed by our tax dollars. The conditions they are running from, Doctors without Borders tells us, are comparable to those of war. Kelly had gone to the border as soon as the news hit about children being separated from their families in detention centers. "I can't stop thinking about those babies," she told me. "I just have to go." But Kelly finds inspiration even in these dark times. She tells me about the community she witnessed there and the love and care those seeking refuge have for one another. She tells me about the border agents, their hostilities and aggression, and the courage these people meet them with. "They're the local peace economy," she tells me. "They are exercising all of the values we need to have to survive these challenges."

I will later be told about what happens behind the scenes — how various agencies show up like cartels, government militias and border agents, and how these various entities coordinate the separation of these people, of children from families, women from men — some murdered, some trafficked; some children, like under the policies of residential schools, are farmed out to American families.

It hadn't been that long ago that Kelly had visited me in Copenhagen to celebrate the publication of my book and to share her own, *Until the Streets of the Hood Flood with Green*, documenting the beginning of her work with the Electric Smoothie Lab Apothecary (TESLA). Based in Oakland for over ten years, she's been engaged in her TESLA project, modeled after the direct action of the Black Panthers. Kelly's goal is to get the nutrients straight to the community. No corporate structures/intermediaries; just plain, localized, personal activism whereby she makes smoothies and chats with her community about the various nutritional benefits her smoothies provide. Through TESLA, Oakland students can now work at a smoothie bar where they also do silk screen printing.

The summer before, she had traveled with me to Berlin for Alanna Lockward's Black Body Politics (BE.BOP) — what would be, unbeknownst to everyone, our last meeting with Lockward, who unexpectedly passed in early 2019, right before I embarked on my trip. Kelly traveled with me first to Birmingham, and then to Berlin. Now here we were, some months after, meeting up in Los Angeles as we had planned.

Kelly's lineage includes a father who sharecropped as a child but would go on to work with one of the leading advertising companies in America. "That's when they started targeting the Black middle class as a consumer market," she'd tell me, mentioning the short 1954 film *The Secret to Selling the Negro*. In this film, the narrator says, "It's a well-known fact that negro customers are influenced by the opinions of others." She'll tell me about the day her father, a major ad executive, tried to explain to her the complexities of selling. "It's like boiling a frog," he told her and went on to explain the slow, tragic inevitable death that will befall the frog. She tells me how this analogy was enough to make her cry. Her father shook his head. "Never mind," he said, realizing the nature of her heart. "This meeting is over. You'd never survive in advertising."

Kelly was born in Chicago, and split her time between there, New York and Connecticut. She remembers family dinners that included neighborhood children from around the globe, and how her mother would tell her that she was a home run. "They not ready for you!" she'd lovingly tell her little daughter. Her mother, Betty Ann, was a homemaker, and greatly influenced Kelly in her understanding of the many intersections of oppression and the importance of cultivating joy, instilling in her the legacy of kindness.

Kelly's mother passed in 2005. I once asked her what the best lesson she ever learned from her mother was. "I remember I came home from school one day. We had a history lesson about slavery, which got me all riled up. So I went home and used the word 'cracker.'"

"Oh, I see," her mother said, looking at her. "You're becoming like them." She told her that they couldn't fight racism with racism. "It's a valuable lesson," Kelly says as she proceeds to heat up some tortillas, "because if you can't talk to White folks, then the battle is over."

I once had the privilege to interview an octogenarian who lived in Florida and it was one of the most interesting interviews I had encountered. My subject was born in Alabama but had moved to Florida as a young wife with her new husband, who was also from the same town as she. They lived on a fruit farm and worked as fruit pickers up and down the east coast, according to the various seasons. "We always traveled as a family, and insisted that we all lived together," she told me. "We knew that there were horrible things that could happen to fruit pickers, so we stuck together," she said with no small amount of pride resonating from her voice.

She and her family ended up doing well for themselves. She told me how she was able to go on to become a nurse and of her first day working. "My first patient was so rude to me. When she saw me, she immediately screamed that she did not want a N-word nurse. I was shocked and went to get my boss." I couldn't imagine such a thing, the indignity of it all!

"I told my boss what had happened," she said in that proper way many of our elders speak. "My boss went into the room to the patient. She was in there for a long time. Finally she came back and told me I could return to my duties with that patient. The patient didn't say a word to me, she was even nice."

"Til this day, I don't really know what my boss said to her."

"But weren't you angry?" I asked, sitting in my own rage about the story. Thinking about the indignities that our elders and ancestors were forced to endure.

"No," she said to me, calmly. Something shifted inside of me; I was interested.

"As a nurse, I'm there to take care of people who are sick. I know that when I'm sick, I'm not my best. I know that when I attend to my patients, they're not at their best either." It was at that moment that I understood the power of maintaining one's dignity in the face of discrimination. Maintaining one's dignity could look many different ways. It could mean extending a great amount of grace to the sick, as in my interviewee's experience. For others, I suppose, it could mean throwing a Molotov cocktail.

Kelly is all heart, as her beautiful, open face attests. With both feet firmly planted on the ground and a being that insists on the transformational dynamic of love (I know this is how she lives, for I have been with her), she has become a capable teacher to me. It is one thing to talk about community and a completely other thing to participate in it. How do we relate to each other, support each other in these neoliberal times? How do we dismantle the ego, the narcissism that has had to be developed, to "survive" in these times? These are all questions worth asking.

I first met Kelly in the mid-Nineties when she was in the throes of creating the iconic *Freedom Rag*, a magazine that garnered the respect of everybody. When I first heard of TESLA (and still to this day), I felt inspired by the direct action of her project. Although this settler colony is supposedly one of the wealthiest countries in the world, thirty-eight million people faced hunger in 2020. TESLA is about autonomy, starting with our bodies. Learning about the agency that we have access to in regards to our health is vital.

Kelly is instrumental in my healing journey. I feel honesty, love and safety in my friendship with her that's been integral to both of our growth. Kelly doesn't call me out; she calls me in with love and patience. She conjures my grandmother's spirit, the spirit of my childhood hero Willie Mae, in whose home I was always welcome ("Lesley, you're my girl"), in a way no one else ever has, with so much love and respect, despite my wayward ways.

Through Kelly, I've been introduced to the work of Gabor Maté, Thích Nhất Hạnh and many other inspirational people committed to creating a better world. Together, we listen to old interviews with Angela Davis, Alice Walker, bell hooks and Audre Lorde. I always think about Kelly whenever I come across the Nina Simone clip where she describes "girl talk" — "it was always Marx, Lenin and revolution." Our friendship grants a space to talk about the state of our world, of our hearts and of our souls.

As in my conversations with friends such as Ida and Gillian, Kelly often speaks about the trauma we as Black and Indigenous people may experience in our relationship with the land. She's acutely aware of the importance of returning to plant intelligence — whether it's through her smoothies or various other herbal concoctions. I'm grateful for her sisterhood. There is no judgment in our friendship, only loving space. Kelly encourages me and seems to welcome critical conversations about the state of the world, particularly in connection to the US. Her work and dedication continue to be a source of inspiration for me. I am thankful that I can say she is part of my community.

Together we spend days walking in Echo Park, talking about liberation and making corn tortillas and jicama. Together we make an altar where we hang her pink bandana. "Magic is totally real," it says. With Kelly, I found some spiritual home. Kelly not only talks about community, she also lives it. From her work with TESLA to her participating in various community gardens, doing the hard work of being in a community with others often entails loving call-ins and (as mentioned before) showing up at the border to offer support to those who find themselves attacked by worshippers in the cult of death. "I just don't know," Kelly would one day lament. "What is wrong with us? People seem so, I don't know… in pain."

I also learn of the many struggles that Oakland is experiencing. With rents rising, many poor people and their families have found themselves without housing. "The other day, I saw this little girl come out of a tent," Kelly told me once. "It was in the morning, and I saw how she fixed her little dress before walking. It broke my heart, seeing her come out of that tent."

As Kelly and I load up her car to head back to Oakland, the rains continue to fall. My next stop is San Francisco, which Kelly drives us to in her late father's Chevy HHR. On our way, we stop at Westlake Village to pay our respects to her parents, Charles Curry and Betty A. Curry. As we stand there, I feel so much gratitude for the legacy that Charles and Betty Curry consciously planted in Kelly's soul. Standing there and looking at the plaques that bear their names, I can't help but think about a Neolithic Aztec poem I had heard the scholar Ivan Illich recite. The poem, he told us, was written by a Spaniard, using Spanish letters, but in Nahuatl. The poem, which was written for a god, says:

> For just a fleeting moment, we are lent to each other.
> We live, because you draw us.
> We have color because you paint us.
> And we breathe because you sing us.
> But for just a fleeting moment, we are lent to each other.
> Because we erase ourselves, like a drawing,
> Even one made in obsidian.
> We lose color, as even the quetzal,
> The beautiful green bird, loses its color.
> And we lost our sound and our breath,
> As does even the water's song.
> For just a fleeting moment, we are lent to each other.

I had been to San Francisco a few times, but never to Oakland, and never over an extended period. However, this will change in a few months when I fly over from New York during the height of the pandemic. Through Kelly, I learn about Oakland's rich political history. As we drive through the rain along the Pacific coastline, Kelly tells me about the deep historical roots of resistance in Oakland. Aside from being the birthplace of the Black Panthers, it was also one of six cities across the country where the Pullman Porters conducted their strike after World War II, and how this marked the beginning of the country's labor movement. Oakland was also the site of Bruce Lee's second martial arts school, with Seattle being the home of his first.

Kelly drives in from Oakland to pick me up from the tiny house I booked in San Francisco for the night, and takes me to the airport.

"I'll see you soon!" we promise each other, although we both have no idea what the future holds for us, or even for the world. I board the Alaska Airlines plane to Portland, and sit back with a feeling of much gratitude.

5.

America is a Eurocentric, fundamentalist settler state

I had never been to Portland, Oregon, before. And I was also excited to visit with my friend and former Flux roommate Christopher Yarrow. Christopher is tall and has a face that is wide and open like his heart. We were able to catch up and I learned he was now playing the washboard in his father's band when he tours. His father is a Sixties music icon. "But other than that," he said, "I'm focused on healing myself and my family."

While visiting Christopher, I learned that he and his family had prioritized their healing — both personal and familial. I learned of his family members who are actively working with native communities and the #landback movement. It was inspiring to hear about and gave me hope about my own family's healing, as well as the world's. Imagine if we all disengaged with the system to focus on ourselves, each other and the earth? To heal? I was particularly inspired by his family's commitment to healing the wounds of colonization with their native relatives. It also gave me hope regarding how various historical wounds could be addressed if this was indeed the day's order.

Although it had now been two years since my ayahuasca experience, a considerable part of this journey I had embarked on was connected to integrating the information I received then into my process of healing and living. Part of this healing meant that I had come to terms with the fallout my family and issues related to home had caused in my life. For me, "home" obviously wasn't just one place. And although spiritually I wanted to be home no matter where I found myself, it was an exercise that I sometimes did not excel at. Sure, there were many times throughout my life when I felt a deep connection to home: this occurred in Copenhagen, Brooklyn and of course in Trinidad. But the truth is, I hadn't had that feeling in years.

Part of this journey was about learning to be grounded no matter where I found myself. I ensured this by always booking a place with a kitchen. Cooking was the ritual that I tended to the most. I found the process comforting — ginger reminding me of my childhood with my grandmother, the sweetness of sautéed onions bringing back memories of Coney Island. Of course, I had my usual go-to dishes: curry, dahl or beans, and rice. In addition, I often travel with my spices and herbal teas and, while visiting, made a pot of dahl for dinner

I had learned from the photographer and Black Portlanders' creator Intisar Abioto that Oregon was once a Whites-only utopia before it became a state. A *National Geographic* article by Nina Strochlic confirms that settlers in Oregon were against slavery as it negatively impacted their ability to earn a decent living. If Black people were allowed to live there, they reasoned, their enslavement would lower the wages of Whites. Another reason, just as important, was that they feared that Blacks and Native Americans would consolidate their power and threaten their monopoly over land. And there was a lot of land. In 1850, the Oregon Donation Land Act was passed by the US Congress. It offered up to 320 acres of free (stolen) land in the territory to any White settler who would cultivate it — an offer not extended to Native Americans, African Americans or Hawaiians. Talk about living off government handouts; this is how the West was won.

Chris helped me organize an event in Portland at Stacks. I invited Intisar Abioto to share the stage with me. Accompanying us that evening was the poet jayy dodd, whose poetry and performance rocked the entire venue. dodd is the author of *Mannish Tongues* and *The Black Condition ft. Narcissus*.

While in Portland, I had a visit from Kathy Jetnil-Kijiner. Jetnil-Kijiner's work focuses on the climate crisis and its threat to the Marshall Islands. According to the US Geological Survey, some of the Marshall Islands will be submerged by 2035. Drinking water will become scarce as saltwater will contaminate their aquifers, which will lead to the Marshallese having to become climate refugees. Like most climate threats, the threat is reversible. But according to an article in the *Conversation*, France has impeded the nation's ability to invest in any of the programs that could alleviate this threat, forcing them instead to depend on foreign aid.

I have often used Jetnil-Kijiner's work in my classroom — her poem "Anointed," made into a short film by Dan Linn in 2018, which can be seen on YouTube, brings me to tears every time I listen to it. After the Second World War, the US tested sixty-seven nuclear weapons on the Marshall Islands. Two decades later, we learn from the intro to the film, contaminated waste was collected and dumped in a crater on Runit Island in Enewetak Atoll.

"Who gave you the power to burn?" Jetnil-Kijiner asks as images of a boat, the Pacific and her fellow islanders flash across the screen. "You were a whole island once;" she continues, "who remembers you beyond your death?"

After Portland, it was finally time to fly to New York — I had an event there in mid-January — then to Johns Hopkins University, and then I'd fly out to Trondheim, Norway, where I had been invited to give a keynote speech.

6.

The pandemic
is a portal...[3]

When I landed in New York and drove home, to my mother's apartment in Brooklyn, in the light of the rising sun, I saw the skyline of brick and concrete that seemed to have conquered the land. But I know that we humans can never build that everlasting monument; even the trees and the plants we so arrogantly call weeds laugh at us, although they still love us and patiently await the arrival of our collective recall.

When I left Copenhagen, I didn't have any real plan other than the itinerary that my publicist and I were able to string together with not that much time. I didn't mind, however. I knew I needed to slow down and take care of myself. My last job had done me in; I was free to investigate a new way forward. Was moving back to the States what would work for me? Could I see myself living in a city as large as New York, when even Copenhagen struck me as too much on most days, especially since I've longed to leave city living?

But by the time I arrived in New York on this cold, sunny February morning, I was ready for the city whose pavements were the pathways of my youth.

When my mother called me, I hadn't been in New York for too long. "Mammy isn't doing too well; she is going to the hospital."

---

3   Title from Arundhati Roy's 2020 essay.

***

I had just returned from a birthday visit with my sister in Pennsylvania, and I had just turned forty-eight. My sister Shelley, my North Star, lives in a small town not too far from New York, tucked in the woods. She is everything I aspire to be: reasonable. If I had the chance to choose one other person to be stranded somewhere with, I'd pick her — no doubt about it. During the NYC blackout of 1977, my five-year-old self jumped into my sister's arms, where she held me for the entire duration of the night, never letting me go. Her home, full of crafting material, books and knickknacks, has been one of the few constants in my life. My sister has my father's slender fingers, her hair recalls various continents, and as she grows older, she is beginning to resemble my mother more and more.

At this point, there had been reports about the coronavirus in Wu Han, but no sign that it would ever become what it did just a few days later. It wasn't until I returned to my mother's house in Brooklyn that I began to realize the seriousness of the situation. At the time, I was in a bit of a gray area — I had by now realized that I wanted to return to Denmark, at least for the time being. I had a place in the countryside, and I couldn't think of anywhere I'd rather be than close to my son, my cats and nature. I had been on the road since leaving Copenhagen in January 2019, including a trip back to Denmark and flights to Norway, Paris and Finland. Although I love to travel, it was time to settle down, if just for a moment, as it was now March of 2020.

At first, when I realized the pandemic was looming, I wanted to return to Trinidad. Gillian and I exchanged messages, but by the time I attempted to buy a ticket, Trinidad and Tobago had closed its borders. I couldn't return.

It may sound counterintuitive now, but when I originally left Copenhagen, it was a way for me to make my way back toward a more healthy and balanced state. I needed a break. Being on the road seemed like a great solution — I could do it at my own pace; and between freelancing, I would focus on therapy, eating better, quitting negative habits and getting to understand better where I felt I belonged on this planet. All of these things I had done up to this point: I was just starting with a therapist in March, before the pandemic. I had worked my way off smoking cigarettes and drinking alcohol. I felt like my body needed my support — so I strove to feed it only healthy things and to take rest seriously. I didn't have anything if I didn't have my health.

Up to the point when everything shut down in New York, throughout the rest of the States and even over much of the world, I thought things couldn't get any worse. It was at my mother's small dining-room table that I realized I would be stuck in the apartment she shared with her partner. I felt a heavy pit in my stomach. Would I survive this pandemic?

7.

Cliffrose Convergence

The journey of healing is not an isolated affair. It wasn't just about me — it is also about my relationships. It's about my friendships, my colleagues, my child and my own family. But how do you heal if you have neither language nor tools? When accessing care has become institutionalized, with corporations and governments elbowing their way into sacred spaces to pick up where we have been broken?

The previous April, I was invited to the Cliffrose Convergence to give the keynote address. Cliffrose Convergence, held at the Frantz Fanon Community Center in Prescott, was a three-day gathering of anti-fascist organizers across the Southwest. We gathered to network, strategize and mobilize around issues, to build networks and to continue to dialogue on resurgent fascism under global capitalism, colonialism, imperialism and the many ways these systems manifest in our respective communities. It was at this convergence that a few things came together for me.

Here, I could connect specific dots regarding my journey and what is happening on a more significant, collective level. To be able to gather with others and discuss themes such as colonization, racism, immigration, addiction and many other issues was healing in of itself.

I was very inspired by the organizers and participants at this event. Students and community activists came out those few days we spent together in the sun as we exchanged knowledge and experiences. It was an awesome experience to get to meet so many people, of all ages, engaging across issues for social change.

I had been invited by some students from Prescott College. which is a small liberal arts college in the town of Prescott ("Pres'kit"), Arizona, the original home of the Yava Pai and Apache nations. I had never been to Arizona before, but it didn't take long to figure out I was in a state that allowed open carry — the practice of visibly carrying a firearm in public. Arizona, like every other part of Turtle Island, is occupied territory. I would soon learn that there was a pro-Trump march every morning in the city.

I shared an Airbnb with the Bronx hip-hop activist group Rebel Diaz, composed of two brothers, Gonzalo (G1) and Rodrigo (Rodstarz), who have roots in Chile. One night, as we all chilled in the Victorian-inspired living room, smoking blunts and talking, Gonzalo told me the fascinating story of his uncle, Victor Toro. From this story, I learned more about migrations, the overthrow of democratically elected presidents to install military dictatorships throughout Abya Yala and how empire works.

8.

Victor Toro

"Victor Toro was locked up with my dad," G1 tells me, "in the mid-1970s in Chile." G1 has a head full of cornrows, just like his brother. He explains that Toro and his father were members of the Revolutionary Movement of the Left, or MIR (*Movimiento de Izquierda Revolucionaria*) — a Chilean socialist group. MIR was known to finance its work through bank robberies, something that G1 tells me Victor later testified in court he never participated in. "Victor organized working people," I am told. "That was his talent."

On 11 September 1973, the democratically elected government of president Salvador Allende was overthrown by a CIA-sponsored coup and replaced with the Pinochet dictatorship. This forced Victor, along with G1's father, to go into hiding — anyone associated with the overthrown government was now in grave danger. Unfortunately, they were both eventually found, arrested and interned in a series of camps where they were tortured.

G1 and Rodstarz's father, however, was released after three years. "He received refugee status in Europe and then eventually went to the US where I was born; my older brother was born in their Europe refugee phase, in London, England."

But Victor Toro's exile from Chile, I am told, was a lot different. He was one of the prominent leaders of the MIR. He was the leader that had the most support in the poorest popular sectors throughout all of Chile. G1 tells me that the MIR had been very middle class, "in the spirit of Che being a doctor and Fidel being a lawyer. But Victor, he was like the hood connect for the party." And this is why, I am told, he was considered a threat to the Pinochet government. "He once mobilized three, five thousand people to reclaim the land. They set up shanty housing and demanded housing reform. This is the sort of support he could galvanize amongst people regularly."

According to a *Time* article, Victor's torture included repeatedly being bound to a metal bed frame and being shocked. In 1977, he was released at the same time as the duo's father. But when he left Chile, the military government declared him dead. They even issued a death certificate for him. "Victor believes that this was a message that if he returned, he could disappear."

And there were many disappearances; according to some estimates, as many as 3500 people. But there was also another reason for the declaration of Victor Toro's death. "Even though Victor had been released and was leaving Chile, the military junta had planned on killing him overseas." This military junta was officially called Operation Condor, and it was a coordinated effort between the military government of Chile and other military governments throughout Latin America that had been installed by the US. These governments coordinated with each other to kill various leftists from Latin America who had fled their countries. I have been told about the case of Pinochet's leading opponent, Orlando Letelier. Letelier was living in exile in the US when he, along with his co-worker and husband, was murdered by a car bomb in Washington, D.C., planted by the Pinochet military government.

"They did that shit here, in the US. So Victor leaves Chile, and this is a man on the run." G1 explains that Victor, a man of revolution, went and participated in revolutionary processes in Cuba, Nicaragua and throughout Latin America, helping to lead different social movements and to train other leaders. He eventually made it to Mexico, where he and his wife and daughter were granted asylum. However, he felt vulnerable, suspecting that his life was still at risk from the Pinochet regime, so he decided to go to the US.

He eventually settled down in the Bronx, NY. "I saw here the third world that I had come from," he said in a *New York Times* article in 2011. G1 explains, "He chose the Bronx, NY, specifically — because it was the poorest congressional district in the United States. He felt that if he was going to be doing work politically in the US, that's where he wanted to be."

In those days, like so many other locations across the country and the world, the Bronx was filled with the woes of economic depression: drugs and gangs. "This man dropped out of school in the third grade and is an autodidact. He taught himself how to read to learn about the world." He made it to the Bronx in the early Eighties, where all sorts of cultural movements emerged from Black and Brown communities, like hip-hop. He supported these movements through his famous cultural and political center, which he established in the Mott Haven section of the Bronx called La Peña. He threw himself into local activism, helping to organize unlicensed street vendors, staging music and arts events, and providing a meeting place for immigrants from Mexico, the Dominican Republic and Honduras.

"When my brother and I arrived in New York in the early 2000s, this man who wasn't our blood but we always knew as our uncle, that lived in New York, that had been locked up with our dad, well… we get to start building with him on a daily level.

"As an elder, he did many things that many elders don't do regarding handing over resources, handing over connects, infrastructure, letting us take leadership. That speaks to who he was, who he is and his political line. It's about people power, and that hasn't changed since his days of activism in Chile in the Seventies."

But things were about to change. "So, fast forward to 2007. Victor is riding on an Amtrak train. He's attending conferences on immigrant rights in several cities. This was under the second Bush presidency, the end of the Bush years. On the way to upstate New York, ICE raids the Amtrak train he is riding on. At that time — they still do it now — but at that time, ICE was doing these random raids, on trains and buses, because they know that's how immigrants who don't have papers travel." ICE, Immigration and Customs Enforcement, not only targets these buses, they also target mostly Black or brown passengers. They ask for your papers. "The only document Victor had on him was his expired Chilean passport. He ain't got no papers, so Victor got locked up." I couldn't help but recall similar tactics I had witnessed in Denmark — both on buses and trains.

At first, G1 tells us, he was facing a typical immigrant case: "He didn't have no papers, he was in this country, and so technically, unlawfully. But one of these young district attorneys wanted to style himself as a young Giuliani and make a name for himself. He digs up Victor's name and realizes his past as somebody that was a militant. As someone who was targeted by the Pinochet regime."

Somehow, this immigration case, even though it stayed in immigration court, became almost like a terrorism case. It was no longer about Victor being in the States with or without documents, but was about his past as a leader of the MIR in

Chile. They wanted to criminalize him and his character, and called not only for his immediate deportation but also for him to be brought up on terrorism charges.

What followed, I'm told, was a crazy trial that lasted about seven years, in which the same government that had facilitated the Chilean government's repression, incarceration, torture and murdering of people, and which had caused Victor to be imprisoned, tortured and exiled, tried him again, in court, thirty or forty years later.

"The trial consisted of crazy questions: 'What's your opinion of Fidel Castro?'" G1 tells me that they would attend the trial along with all the other young people from the 'hood. "There was a mad, funny mix of audience members. There were, like, old White leftists who had supported the Chilean cause back in the day. Young homies were coming with us from the Bronx. And so we're all there, supporting.

"It was wild because we got a straight school lesson on how two-faced interrogation is from the empire." Victor was able to flip the tables on the prosecutors, and in so doing, he exposed the role of the US government in the coup, the subsequent dictatorship in Chile and his having to flee his own country.

"More information has come out in the last couple of years through WikiLeaks about Operation Condor, this plan of coordination of military juntas throughout Latin America, plotting to kill leftist revolutionaries, and documents about the US's direct involvement in the coup in Chile and the dictatorship.

"Victor's logic was: Number one, how will you deport me back to a country that has already declared me dead? That has a constitution that is the same constitution that was created under the military dictatorship; even if that dictatorship is officially gone, the military is still in power. Number two, they would probably kill me if they were ever given the opportunity, still, thirty, forty years later. Three, you want me to have entered the US legally when I came in the Eighties, when the US itself was aiding and abetting Operation Condor. All of these military juntas targeting leftist revolutionaries, which the US had an interest in supporting again." His logic was sound.

Victor initially lost the case, but then he appealed. The judge denied his asylum request, saying his homeland was now safe and democratic since 1990. But she also rejected the government's claim that he had engaged in terrorist activities. According to the *Times*, she even seemed sympathetic, expressing disbelief that he never sought asylum or a green card in all this time in the US, especially since his wife and child were both legal residents. He spoke of his distrust of the US government for its support of the Pinochet regime, and explained that he didn't want to risk deportation. Instead, he had waited for a change in immigration laws. Although he didn't officially win the case, he did receive a stay of deportation. He wasn't deported but was allowed to stay in the US, which G1 says "is kind of like jail because he can't leave. But he can live out the rest of his years here. He's already in his mid-seventies and continues doing his thing in the Bronx. He's like the mayor of his block. Everybody knows Victor because he does so much for the neighborhood. He's a dude who made gang truces in the Eighties and Nineties. He would bring coffee to the day laborers who would gather on one of the street corners by the gas station to work for meager wages throughout the day. He'd come six in the morning and bring them fucking coffee, just do acts of solidarity that were about building his hood. So he still does that.

"The gist of it is that the US tried to flip the script and create a terrorism case out of an immigration case and, in doing so, exposed themselves for the crimes that the US has done throughout Latin America."

I learned so much during my stay at Prescott. The Cliffrose Convergence demonstrated the power we had as people through activism. There were many interesting discussions and panels, one of which was about the role of adverse childhood experiences — ACEs — in determining life outcomes as well as harm reduction in addiction and what that could look like. Throughout the convergence, as well as all throughout my trip, I thought about my students back in Denmark, and how much their lives would benefit from trauma-informed care.

9.

Broken land

It was that time of year when Brooklyn lindens blossom — their flowers flood the air with their scent of honey — when I turned to Queen Afua for pandemic advice. I was desperate and had often found comfort in her in the past. I found a video of her in which she addressed the pandemic. The first thing she said was that, if we wanted to survive Covid-19, we would have to forgive our mothers.

Bet. I can do this. I'm close to fifty and determined.

I was going to nurture my mother with healthy foods and spend loving time with her. We were going to get through this pandemic together. I reasoned that there had to be some great cosmic reason that we had ended up together during this time. And it had to be more than *90-Day Fiancé*, right?

Despite my age, and accompanied by the constant noise from the eternally blaring television (from which come sound bites of Wendy asking, "How you doing?") and my mother's general pandemic anxiety, I found being an obedient daughter difficult.

"We were close when you were a baby," she told me one day, in a rare moment of tenderness.

At the beginning of the pandemic, we hungrily ate up the news to find out about this mysterious virus. As the reports revealed that New York City was now the world's epicenter of the pandemic, I could feel the blood drain from my body. I was petrified. I did not want to die six thousand miles away from my son. I did not want to get sick — I couldn't afford to — I didn't even have health insurance. I didn't want to be in New York. I tried to escape. *I should have known better than to travel to the States while Trump is president*, I groaned to myself, knowing full well that there was more to it than that.

I began reading as much as possible about the virus, trying to get my head around what I could do to keep myself and my community healthy. I noticed that, in all of the news programs I listened to or watched, there was nothing about how we could protect ourselves or boost our immune systems. There was an ever-growing tally of deaths, grim pictures of mass graves and frantic tones from newscasters. Images of the city that never sleeps brought to its knees. "This is worse than 9/11," I heard many New Yorkers say. I thought about all the shuttered stores I had seen throughout New York and all the other urban centers I had visited in the States before the pandemic. We were already in trouble — what would this pandemic mean for us, and myself, economically? The streets were emptied as in an eerie Hollywood film. I also was not the only one to notice that the lockdowns came in a year that followed two of the most politically active years globally: 2018 and 2019 saw demonstrations from Ecuador to Chile to the Middle East and France.

I made a batch of fire cider, which I shared with my household and others in the community. It was the early stages of the pandemic, and even the air seemed suspect. It was crazy. My mother and I decided that I would be the one to go shopping.

"You can't keep watching this," I told my mom one day. She was lying on the bed, her arms crossed against her chest, a worried expression on her face. She was rubbing her feet like she always had throughout my childhood, expressing nervous energy she had yet to manage.

"You're right," she agreed, and turned it off. My mom usually went to a senior center, which had been shut down at the onset of the pandemic. Without this, my mother had no social network other than her phone, which she seemed to now desperately cling to. I understood.

I tried to tell her in the least nagging way possible (I failed miserably at this) that her mind will disintegrate if she doesn't use it. Not even a year before, my mother became gravely ill and was in a coma for two weeks. Since her miraculous recovery, however, I noticed that she seemed more forgetful and often repeated specific stories. And ever since she'd lost her mother, I couldn't help but notice that she seemed more fragile.

My mother is beautiful, and this beauty has always been something she appreciates. She's always been a fan of make-up, hair relaxers, dyes and hard plastic hair rollers; it wasn't until recently that I had even seen my mother's natural hair. She also attempted to hand down her beauty standards to my sister and me. My sister never did straighten her hair, always choosing to wear her hair naturally. I, on the other hand, went through a phase where I dabbled in the crack cream, wore hard plastic rollers to bed every night and attempted to fit my mother's version of what "pretty" meant. Sometimes it felt unbearable to hear her repetitive stories, but I would whisper Queen Afua's words under my breath and usually go for a walk to hang out with the trees of Brooklyn.

I made pots of ginger, turmeric and garlic tea, which I seasoned with a pinch of ground black pepper and a dash of lemon juice. When I went to the grocery store, which we had to line up for as only a few were allowed in at a time, I was shocked to see all of the fresh produce still in abundant supply while shelves of processed food stood empty. Folks didn't realize that we needed healthy, wholesome, fresh foods in the face of a pandemic.

I also started to crave sardines. I have never been a fan of sardines. Fish in a can! Anything in a can tends to turn me off — but from somewhere deep inside my body, I wanted sardines. I bought a few cans and prepared them with onions, tomatoes and coriander. I ate sardines every day for about a month. Curious about this craving, I learned that sardines are one of the best food sources of vitamin D, a vitamin that many Covid-19 patients are found to have deficient levels of, and which is integral to our immune system.

I'd often hang out at "the mountain" — a building full of island men — with Jacob, a Jamaican artist who handmakes intricate leather purses and various clothing styles. The crew was eclectic and included many musicians, and with the sound of Burning Spear in the background, I heard stories of stowaways on banana boats coming to America. Sometimes I would even prepare food there — fried plantains that we'd eat on the side, vegan oxtails (yes! It's possible!), rice and peas.

While I was in New York, the symptoms of another (yet familiar) pandemic reared their head. Before the pandemic officially hit in March, there had been the hunter-styled execution of Ahmaud Arbery. Arbery, who was only twenty-five, was murdered by three White men while he was out jogging. Then there was the case of the two Coopers in Central Park, one a White woman (Amy) who threatened to call the cops on the other, Christian (no relation). Then there was the murder of Breonna Taylor. In her own home. While she slept. And still, no justice has been served. Only two months into the pandemic, on 25 May 2020, Minneapolis police officer Derek Chauvin, using a tactic developed by the Israeli police, knelt on the neck of George Floyd, a forty-six-year-old Black man, for nine minutes and twenty-nine seconds, murdering him over an alleged counterfeit $20 bill.

Video of Chauvin continually kneeling on the dying Floyd's neck is brutal. He seems indifferent. The video of Floyd's murder reminded us of the history of state violence that this country has always used against non-White and, in this case, Black Americans. So while we battled the uncertainty of the pandemic, activists and regular citizens took to the streets, from Brooklyn to Portland, Oregon, which had the longest-running protests.

A month after Floyd's very public lynching, a young man was brutally murdered on the sunny Danish island of Bornholm. Phillip Mbuji Johansen was a young twenty-eight-year-old engineering student, and had just graduated from school. Of Danish and Tanzanian roots, he visited his mother on the idyllic island of Bornholm. His murderers are two White, young, Danish men. Despite one of the perpetrators having a swastika tattoo on his leg along with a history of far-right affiliations, the court system had determined that this murder — which included injuries to the victim's spinal cord that are in accordance with his having received a knee to the neck like George Floyd — was not racially motivated. To add insult to injury, the brothers used as part of their defense the story that Johansen had sexually assaulted their mother. In white supremacy, there is no swifter justification to execution as a Black man accused of sexually assaulting a White woman.

10.

Writing is
my home

I began to attempt to write something out of this space.
Whenever I write, I read. The only rhyme and reason for my
reading is my interest. I try to see how it connects to other
things I have been thinking about. I read *The Myth of Race,
the Reality of Racism* by Mahmoud El-Kati. El-Kati reminds us
that these "systems of domination, imperialism, colonization,
and racism actively coerce black folks to internalize negative
perceptions of blackness, to be self-hating." He writes that
"the monotonous and senseless murder of Black people by
'whites' over many generations, does not stigmatize 'whites'
as violent. Power is responsible for obscuring reality." He
writes about the myth of race that springs from the human
imagination and our "penchant for categorizing, cataloging,
and pigeonholing life." Race, he reminds us, is unscientific
as it "violates the first laws of science, which are observation
and consistency." He goes into the systemic nature of it and
how every level of our society is affected by its construction,
economic, social, political, cultural and spiritual.

I reread bell hooks' *Killing Rage,* in which she begins with
the truth: "It is painful to think long and hard about race and
racism in the United States." In the book, she looks into the
role of denial as a "cornerstone of white European culture."
She writes about the repeated assault and harassment that
Black people suffer from White people in a White supremacist

culture, how the state condones the violence and how necessary this violence is to "the maintenance of racial difference."

She encourages us, as Black people, to be unashamed of our rage, to use it "as a catalyst to develop critical consciousness to come to fill decolonized self-actualization," but cautions that such a person "had no real place in the existing social structure." She writes about the dangers of silence and reminds us, "Rage is at times a useful and constructive response to exploitation, oppression, and continued injustice."

For hooks, White denial of the violence of White supremacist, capitalist, patriarchal culture has reached "epidemic pathological proportions," which cannot be resolved until it is recognized "that white supremacy is rooted in pathological responses to difference." White supremacy, hooks writes, "is frightening; it promotes mental illness and various dysfunctional behaviors on the part of whites and non-whites. It is the real and present danger — not black rage."

I particularly like what she wrote about radical feminism and, as Michele Wallace wrote in her seminal *Black Macho and the Myth of the Black Superwoman*, how Black liberation was betrayed through the adaptation of White patriarchal behavior. "Revolutionary feminism is not anti-male." It includes an understanding of how the lives of Black men are threatened "by their uncritical absorption and participation in patriarchy." hooks notes how one of radical feminism's most significant challenges is the presence of bourgeois values — whereby the rights of middle-class women are valued more than those of poor Black women. She has said that this group of activists "offer little zeal to challenge and counter the denigration of poor single mothers, especially Black females."

These words brought me back to Gillian Goddard and Kelly Curry, both of whom I was lucky enough to have had many conversations with about class, gender, sexuality and race issues. For Kelly, her mother was the ultimate teacher in this respect: "When I think about all the things my mother could have done if she wasn't a stay-at-home mother…" Kelly confides to me one day, continuing on to say that middle-class expectation suppressed her talents at a time when she could not work. Gillian told me about the moment she realized that she had been programmed all her life to get as far away as possible from those she came from, "poor Black women." These stories help me reflect upon my own experiences with class, although I had never considered it in this way until very recently.

The truth is, I've been so interested in understanding race and racism that I never really took the time to understand how class stratifications impact the societies of which I have been a part. In Trinidad and Tobago, class was always ever-present, usually encoded in skin color. This was something my US passport seemed to protect me from — as being able to leave is considered a privilege and provides access to possible economic mobility.

In the many years I have lived in Denmark, I came to see that the idea that Denmark was a classless system was a myth. I could see how those who migrate here would always mainly occupy the lower strata of this society, forming an underclass.

I had noticed that the term "White supremacy" seemed inadequate. As Nelson Mandela once said, "White supremacy implies black inferiority," and I discovered the term "Eurocentric fundamentalism," coined by Danish-Palestinian poet Yahya Hassan. It seems so fitting.

I read Patrisse Khan-Cullors and asha bandele's *When They Call You a Terrorist* and learned that, in the US, someone can allege that you said something threatening to them, which caused them to fear for their life, and you can then be charged with terrorism. In the book, her brother, who has a history of mental health issues, finds himself in the criminal justice system — something that many poor people who don't have the resources for private care often find themselves in. She suggests that "the drug war, the war on gangs, has been no more than a forced migration project. From my neighborhood in LA to the Bay Area to Brooklyn, Black and Brown people have been moved out as young white people build exciting new lives standing on our bones. The drug war was ethnic cleansing."

When my grandmother was in the hospice, I had agreed to attend the eightieth birthday dinner of a Puerto Rican matriarch in uptown Manhattan. I was invited by her son, someone who had been following my work for quite some time. It turns out that he and his sister both knew Marie Brown, my former employer and mentor. While I was at this party — which was filled with tropical plants and featured a table of Puerto Rican and Caribbean cooking, including fried plantains and rice and beans — I was told about the fate of one of her sons. "All the Puerto Rican neighborhoods were flooded with heroin," the sister said to me. "But they didn't do anything until that Kennedy boy died. It was only until he died from an overdose up here that folks woke up to the heroin epidemic that had already devastated our community."

I was taken on a tour of the sister's apartment, which is right below her mother's. She had adorned her walls with figurines of various Catholic saints. "This is what is so powerful about our culture," she said to me, holding a brown-skinned figure of a woman in her hand. "We took our belief systems and put them onto the Catholic system. That's just genius," she said, her enthusiasm matching her conviction. "And that's how our culture has survived."

11.

Trees that grow
in Brooklyn

There is so much birdsong in Brooklyn.

There's a gray bird that sounds like a cat. It's called a gray catbird.

In the quiet of the pandemic streets, I go out and pay attention to all the trees that line the blocks. It's tough for me to get much done during the lockdown. I meditate and exercise. Read. Knit. Sometimes I join Jacob in his workouts at Forte Green Park. We lift weights, run up and down significant steps and do push-ups and jump rope. I don't know how old Jacob is; he won't tell me. But his body is chiseled, and his face shifts from that of a young boy to that of a wise elder in seconds. Born in a Jamaican ghetto, he tells me how he was once shot in the face as a young man. He tells me about the political gangs and memories of growing up with his mother in the countryside. He arrived in New York in the Eighties and has been here ever since. When I ask him if he ever wants to return to Jamaica, he tells me, "You cyah live foreign and then go back with nothing."

In New York, Covid-19 has emptied the usually busy streets of people, but now it's full of hollow Amazon boxes, their smiley insignia taunting passersby, along with the carcasses of rats.

At the beginning of the pandemic, I would walk to Fort Greene Park, enjoying the unusual quiet that had descended on these Brooklyn streets. Aside from the seemingly constant sound of emergency sirens and the usual choral thank-you to our healthcare workers every evening (which included hitting pots and pans and screaming out of our windows, and which I didn't participate in but enjoyed hearing the collective noise of). One day, to my delight, I spy a strawberry patch at the base of a tree in the park.

Spring happens on her own, with not that many to witness the cherry blossoms blooming. The stores, all shuttered, seem eerie. Before the pandemic, this part of Brooklyn — Fort Greene/Clinton Hill/Myrtle Avenue — had already looked like it was under some economic siege. Some restaurants seem to have made it through, though — like Buff Patty, the Jamaican restaurant where my mother and I would often buy roti, which subdued our Trini roti cravings, and a multitude of bodegas.

The sound of birds chirping took on a more prominent presence in the rugged landscape of the city, and I awoke to a litany of birdsong every morning. The linden tree on Ryerson Street, not too far from Myrtle, began pushing out lime-green-colored leaves, and a patch of mint turned up at an abandoned parking lot around the corner. Although there were reports of toilet paper shortages in Manhattan, the residents in my Brooklyn neighborhood quietly accepted the long lines outside the supermarket. The fresh fruits, vegetables and herbs were all there; sometimes the ginger and turmeric would run out, but I soon found a small shop down the street to secure my stash. I made ginger, turmeric, and garlic tea, sipping it throughout the day. I cooked food for myself and my mother: roasted cauliflower, beans and rice and veggie burgers. My mother mainly complained of my healthier food choices, resorting to her cans of vegetables whenever she became tired of my cooking. Gradually, we built a routine whereby I would awake at six, move into the dining room and write at the dining-room table to the sound of birds outside her window. On many days it worked, and on others, like when I finally did reach the end of my rope, the fissures allowed for a putrid sadness and disappointment to erupt into our future.

"You need therapy," I told my mother. "I know." She answered, like a little child caught at something. "Being in an abusive relationship affects everyone involved," I told her, thinking about my habits and behavior. I recalled a conversation I had with Gillian regarding abuse, and the role abusive relationships play in upholding our current social order. How many of us learn to become subservient to the system, through conditioning, whether intentional or not, from our own abusive parents. "What you think about this one?" my mother asked me, shoving a picture in my face of a dress on her phone screen. "Do you think I should get the black or brown one?"

I go out to look at trees and to learn about them. I understand that the most common tree in Brooklyn is the London Plane tree. I know about the tree of heaven, the tree referred to in *A Tree Grows in Brooklyn*, which I finally read; I enjoy it but don't miss the subtle racism of it. I discovered that honey locusts look like trees of heaven and that the latter is, in fact, invasive and quite challenging to get rid of. The irony.

I spot European linden trees, silver-leafed maple, English elm, horse chestnut, weeping willows, silver-leafed poplars, English ash, ginkgoes, and honey locust trees. There's a catalpa growing in the mountain's backyard; it's in full bloom. Its arms stretch from the center of the garden to the very corners of it and keep me in loving protection as its leaves and branches form a canopy over my head, protecting me from the summer sun. One day I spot a northern cardinal, its chatter as bright as its red color. Against the quiet of the Brooklyn streets, I get an idea of what this land was perhaps like before all of this. Across the street from my mother's apartment, someone has hung a banner from their window. "Abolish the Police," it reads.

Linden
Tilia
The tree of abundance
Represents the sacred heart

Linden, Tilia americana

12.

The boxes

One day, as I sat at my mother's glass kitchen table going over notes in my journal, she walked in. "Lesley, what you going to do with those boxes?" I looked at the woman whose smell always takes me back home, and not for the first or last time, recognize myself in her.

That's right, I think, *she told me that I had a few boxes in her basement.*

13.

Excavation
May 2020

I'm sitting in Fort Greene park, and the sun is shining and embracing me with its warmth this May day. A cooling breeze gently brushes past me this way and that. The trees and plants debuted on mostly empty streets. As the cherry trees blossomed, Brooklynites, depending on their socio-economic background, were primarily huddled in home offices, overcrowded apartments or private backyards.

At the beginning of the pandemic, I would sometimes walk the seven or so blocks from Ryerson, on Myrtle, to the park, in great comfort with the company of myself and in the presence of the city I know so well, that borough I was born in, whose pavements I tumbled on in playground fights or that my skinny legs drummed in hours of double Dutch.

It's difficult not to get caught up in the marvel of how much has changed here and how much hasn't. I can't help but notice that, before the pandemic desolation that has now descended, the neighborhood's most recent inhabitants, mostly of European ancestry, now dominate these public spaces, even on the Myrtle Avenue side of the park, which is directly across from the projects. Areas where once little Black and Brown children played have been claimed by dogs, the air of White-settler entitlement stifling. Where do all the Black people go?

One of the annoying things about being from New York is that many project onto you their Hollywood-informed idea of what they think you should be like. The world ends up doing to Americans what we do to the world: prejudging us based on Hollywood depictions. But I do understand why we are perceived the way we are outside our national bubble. I can be all those things others hate about Americans: loud, arrogant, defensive, even narcissistic at times. There is no way for me to escape the historical reality that I was raised in a context that simply was not about my ability to thrive but to survive. The united settler states of America, from its very inception, has had to be loud, arrogant, defensive and narcissistic at times. Just as Europe has fallen in love with her image, so too have all her settler states.

The idea that change is good has been used to usher in presidential victories and even to guide spiritual journeys. I find this concept difficult to believe in when confronted by how much New York has changed. But I must remind myself that this has always been the nature of this world. I think about the recent changes on the horizon on my own mother's street. The rumor has been in the air for over a year that the owner of her building wants to sell. This means that my mother will have to move eventually. My mother is in her seventies, and although the house is falling apart, it's her home, and she doesn't want to leave. Leaving, for her, is a source of anxiety. Her rent is relatively low because she had lived in her apartment for many years. It's high, but for New York it's still cheap.

The person who owns her building also owns two other buildings on that street, meaning that the mountain and the house next to it will have to vacate. All of these tenants have been there for at least ten years. And it's not necessarily even a race thing — the owner is Black.

I guess the part I find disturbing when I return to New York is that the change is difficult to swallow when you see the devastation it has wrought on communities close to you. How can I walk down childhood streets, and accept that nothing is there — nothing living, that is; nothing that reaches out to you in the act of recognition, belonging or welcoming even? Faces from childhood are forever erased; your memories are so strong that they are now like ghosts. But the trees — they have been there all along.

I am here, too. I must pick up the pieces I see strewn about me as I walk these Brooklyn streets — like the amputee in front of the liquor store, who stands there, like a battered bird, with a crumbling paper cup in their hand — and make sense of them.

There is also joy, however. Joy can be accessed by standing on the corner of Willoughby and Ryerson in the sun and seeing the blossoms on a cherry tree. It can be accessed by sitting still as the breeze caresses you lovingly, the four directions bringing its cleansing, its healing.

Joy can be accessed through Jamaica Kincaid's novel *See Now Then*; I was lucky enough to meet her at the Brooklyn Caribbean Literature Festival, and she signed my copy. I even got to chat with her and discover that she is as warm as she is intelligent. I nestle into and find solace in how she dexterously wields her self-awareness, turning it into humor, humor that could only be born out of the ability of the writer not to take herself too seriously, even if she is Jamaica Kincaid.

In this quarantine-era Brooklyn, I am stuck. My flight back to Copenhagen has been canceled twice already. But I am healthy and have escaped the chaos of the virus; I have found a window into the past and the time to peer through it to see how, up till now, I have traversed life.

I'm not sure if I think things happen for a reason or if everything is random chance. But I know that given time (or taking it), one can always wring meaning out of certain events in one's life. I got "stuck" in Brooklyn. It could be the nature of the universe.

My window to the past is in the form of the boxes of my things in my mother's house. The contents of these boxes cover a period of my life I had long forgotten, but unbeknownst to me, I desperately needed to reconnect with.

In these boxes were hundreds of pictures — pictures of an adolescent me in Trinidad; a picture of my father, young, a guitar strapped across his shoulder. There are pictures of my family, together and seemingly happy: Mommy, Daddy, my siblings Gerry, Shelley and I, in a time and space long dissipated into the past, another life. There are pictures of me in Trinidad with friends. Our Providence Girls' Catholic School uniforms look awkward and new as we were still very early in our process of blossoming into who we were becoming.

The sun is shining today despite reports of rain. Today I am sitting in the backyard under a canopy of leaves. I am knitting — or reknitting, as when news hit of the pandemic, I was out of yarn, so I decided to unravel an Icelandic sweater I had attempted years before. It's a two-toned sweater, striped with soft, cream-and-ruby-colored wool. It's the perfect exercise in meditation to have during uncertain times, and I am thankful for this movement of recreation, which grounds me. There is so much birdsong in Brooklyn. The rain finally falls, and there is a breeze. Under the leaves, I remain dry.

As I sorted through my old journals, pictures, letters and report cards, I was able to see patterns in my life in a way that was closed off to me before, because now, instead of darkness when I thought about this past, I had physical evidence of a life once lived. Now, I felt like I could put all these pieces together, and from this, motifs would emerge, and finally I could look myself in the eyes and lay my past to rest by forgiving myself and others and committing never to repeat these mistakes again.

In these boxes were journals running from my last year in Trinidad, when I was fifteen, to right before I left New York, in 1999, to move to Copenhagen.

I even found a letter from my now-deceased grandmother.

It was one she wrote to me while I was at a writing retreat, Norcroft, in Duluth, Minnesota. Written in 1993 — she was seventy-three — it was in response to questions I had asked her about her childhood place.

Not good at writing. Excuse scratches, <u>I'm tired.</u>

Mrs. Hildred Balbirsingh
120A Hall Street
Brooklyn, NY 11205
To: Miss Lesley-Ann Brown
c/o Norcroft
P.O. Box 218
Lutsen, MN 55612

About my youth

I remember growing up in Santa Cruz with my aunt and her children, who were much older than me. The oldest cousin was my godmother. Her name was Christiane Lopez. She loved me very, very much. We had not much material things, but I had love from this particular person. I was told when my brother Nicklis died at age perhaps two years, I was nine months old. Christiana kept me while Ma went to Todd's Road where this child died. Todd's Road is where Paul Lopez bought land and went there to live when Ma mother died. Ma was still a young girl and did not want to leave Santa Cruz to live in a more wooded area. She said they had no church or school and as you know she liked her church.

~~Anyway, it was after not staying with her during~~

This part of the letter with land and Paul Lopez has nothing to do with me or my brother or sisters. Ma was still young.

After her marriage to Pa it was Aunty Baby, my brother and me, nine months old, my nenen, means godmother, and she was Christiana who took me with her back to Santa Cruz while my mother went to bury her son. I never lived with Ma again until I was 13 years old, lived with her and my sisters for six years then got married to daddy 1944 January 23 until now. So that's it.

I turned the thin paper over:

I try my best to write these down for you.

There was church, school, regular games in the school yard. I was always welcome at my older married cousin's. I did a lot of walking, especially climbing hills on the northern range over the hills of five miles, before the Americans made the Maracas road through the mountains in 1942. We spent times at a place estate of my Uncle every August month school vacation where we enjoyed all fresh fruits and vegetables, all fresh oranges, banana, cherries, mangoes, avocado, sugar cane, green vegs, grapes. We had growing fresh fish in abundance, wildmeat, crabs, so many local fruits that I've not seen in the US. During vacation time we took care of the beautiful rose trees around the house.

We were more to church. I made my first communion and confirmation when I was 7 years old all in the same day. We continued being placed in a society called "Children of Mary." We had to keep the grotto clean and procession every first Sunday of the month. I've been going to Cyril's Bay even before I can walk. We enjoyed boat rides in the very deep ocean that once seven of us children with one fisher man went out and was very, very frightening. The weather became terrible bad and I must say only God was with us at that time we hadn't engine on boats it was oars and open fishing boat. The sea was so terrible the waves were coming high above the boat and I thought it would come over us and wash us away. Instead the waves went under the boat. In the meantime my uncle was in a state at the house worried about us down at the beach. We came ashore and had one hour climbing the hills to get to the house. One can just imagine how annoyed my uncle became when he heard we were out at sea in such bad weather. We went out to sea when it was calm and the sea was furious. I had a nice childhood without money. — Hildred

My Dear Les,

Ma's full name — Edwardline Lopez Charles.

She died October 19, 1983, age 90 years. You will have to work out her birth year.

Pa's full name — Andrew Charles. Died Feb. 19, 1974.

Birth March 1. He was xx years old when he died. I know nothing of his parents except that they came from India. What part I don't know. He was born in Trinidad. They never spoke much about their life.

Ma's father — Paul Lopez. Seem like her mother died early, there was not much said about her, never heard her name except for the fact she had loved to bake for her family and neighbors and they grew up on an estate (cocoa estate) which every one at that time lived by.

My full name is Hildred Frances (Charles) Balbirsingh. Was born at Cantaro Village upper Santa Cruz.

Hildred September 17, 1924.

Your grandfather is Ewart Gladstone Balbirsingh, born Feb 5 1919. To Fitzgerald and Beryl Daphney Nunez Balbirsingh.

A whole lot was said about them but never their age. Seems though, that she was young when Ewart was born 1919, she did a lot of embroidery, which is fancy work on cloth, a homemaker. Ewart's father worked at the health dept in Trinidad, after meeting and marrying Beryl. No dates but Ewart was born Feb. 5, 1919, five months after that the couple left for

Canada by boat in those days. I understand they went to Nova Scotia. I cannot spell but you should be familiar with the word. Anyway, he had hoped to be a MD with her helping him by taking a job making children clothes at a factory and like preparing things for new brides making money to help her husband. Unfortunately she died when daddy was three years old. Her love for seeing Ewart again or he ever knowing her was over. But her wishes were that she would be back home in Trinidad with her doctor husband and reunite with her child. She did leave him with her ever loving great aunt Fid whose real name was Fedora Nunez Phipps, sister to George Nunez who was then Ewart's grandfather. Ewart's father managed to come over to the US. He never wrote to them in Trinidad but once after his wife died. So no one knew about him ever again.

Strange enough, not so long ago, maybe before you came to Trinidad, we heard from someone who got in touch with him through letters. He lived right there in Queens around the same place you all once lived. I felt for Ewart when the person mentioned to us about her writing to him, Ewart's father, a nice letter telling him about his son Ewart and his beautiful wife with lovely children and how he had this good job and she herself did good as a principal of a secondary school and if he would like to come to Trinidad. His answer was yes, he accepted. Then she turned on him and wrote him a nasty letter. He did not explain what she said, but I was hurt for daddy as he would be happy to even write to his father. We never asked her for the address. He passed away after all this, and to know that we were so close living in Queens. He did change his name from Balbirsingh. You must know that this person is Ewart's sister.

Fedora Phipps was a true mom to Daddy. She loved him more than anyone could believe, she even spoiled him. She was more of a mother to me and a real grandmother to Beryl, Bernice, Steve and Bev. Only Bev being the last child can't remember her much. Vince came after.

I'm tired writing, it's the best I can do. Do make use of the time and of your thing and don't worry about the past. No evil meant if it anything

only tease. I always say to you you have a face like Penny, and you should
try miss Blk America. I'm sorry if I offended you in any way.
I love you always; god bless, sincerely,
Hildred.

Throughout the years, I amassed a wealth of documentation about my grandmother. I have hours of her on film and audio, and many pictures. But it is this letter, written to me when I was in my mid-twenties and attending my first writer's retreat in Minnesota, that is perhaps the best gift I could have ever received after her transition. I thought this letter was in Denmark, in my mother-in-law's basement. But no, here it was in my box at my mother's house in my grandmother's handwriting.

And the letter recalled that place where she had written to me: I stayed in a house in Duluth, on the shore of Lake Superior. I fell asleep to the sound of waves crashing like the ocean outside my window. I shared a house with two other women, writers from across the US. One was a young mother who seemed grateful for the time away and slept a great deal. The other was a retired teacher from Ohio named Joy. She told me that her parents had wanted to call her Zelda but had changed their minds after the institutionalization of Fitzgerald's wife. Joy failed her driving test three times, but after the third, she told me, she cried and her instructor granted her the license. I applied to attend this retreat based on a novel I have yet to finish, a novel whose central character was based on my grandmother.

In these boxes, I find a faded picture of myself in the second grade. I'm wearing a polyester turquoise dress, with a matching vest. My hair is braided — and from its disheveled look I remember how I would braid my hair myself, as my mother would often complain about the texture of my hair. I have the same big-toothed smile and, if I look closely, I can detect my lifelong lazy eye. I smile back at this portrait of myself as a child. It's been a ride, that's for sure. But here I was — 47. I had survived.

Epilogue
Keiko's garden
June 2020

In Oakland, I stay in a cottage out the back of Keiko's house, which she shares with her son. Keiko Kubo teaches Ikebana — a centuries-old Japanese art of arranging flowers — on Zoom. Keiko is a Nikkei (Japanese American) woman, born and raised in and around Detroit, Michigan. After five years as a college dropout, she moved the Bay Area to finish her degree at UC Berkeley on New Year's Day, 1975, and has lived there ever since. Keiko believes we need to build a world based on a culture of peace, with respect for the planet and all who reside here. She's volunteered decades of work through the American Friends Service Committee, based on gratitude for Quaker support of Japanese people imprisoned in WWII Concentration Camps, and now works with Tsuru for Solidarity, a group started by Nikkei people who were children in those WWII Concentration Camps, to end detention of children and families, as well as at J-SEI, a Japanese Senior and Community Center, including by teaching Ikebana.

Keiko is in her seventies and practices qi dong every other morning. She allows me access to her generous stash of yarn. I will knit five sweaters while I am here. Kelly sometimes visits me at the cottage with her two dogs, Play and Sausage. Many potted plants and trees surround the cottage, with a couple of plum trees producing abundantly since my arrival. There are a few pots of tomato plants in the back and a plentiful supply of succulents. There's a blackberry bramble, one I will pick from and even get my hair caught in while picking the berries. I will spy the various birds as they chatter early in the morning. I will learn that some plants are not so welcome in the state of California: English ivy is an invasive species and one that is discouraged to grow. Kelly is connected to a few gardens in the community, and when she comes by, there's a good chance her hands will be full of sizeable purple-green leaves of kale and lots of different kinds of mint, including chocolate as well as pineapple sage. She usually throws these into her Vitamix, the machine she uses to make smoothies for her community.

My last day in New York was like many others. I awoke around six, dressed, prepared my coffee and sat at the glass kitchen table to begin my daily practice. My mother had awakened irritable that morning. Restless. She sat on her exercise bike and tried to do some exercise, which she rarely does. Her muscles hang flaccid, but she is still a beautiful woman. Her hair is all gray, she has finally stopped dying it red, and she loves to don acrylic clothes that are shiny and silky to the touch.

What would my family have been like if there was no television? There was the television and the world my uncle Steve accessed from it in Trinidad. From morning to night, he would sit, watching television shows from the Fifties, from a time long ago, with characters and storylines that had nothing to do with the rich life he had in the beautiful islands of Trinidad and Tobago. How can the inheritors of such an earthly paradise get trapped reproducing an alien hell? I know the violence under which all nations are born, which twists and contorts our visions into submission. The way the *Andy Griffith Show* jingle filled the otherwise quiet Caribbean air was jarring, almost eerie — the whistle and gaiety of it mocking, even.

My mother, too, is captured by this magnetic box. From the time she wakes up until she falls asleep, the television in her room is on. She's really into Wendy Williams, hungry for the gossip, although it's usually about celebrities too young for her to recognize. This she complains about: "Oh, Wendy, shut up! You boring, girl! Put someone on we know, Nah!"

She also watches *The View*, an American television program that sets a group of women up, panel-like, to give their take on specific subjects like strippers who fall off poles and which features Whoopi Goldberg.

After my mother exercised, she goes to the dining room, where she began to fiddle with her phone. She spends long periods on Facebook and has WhatsApp threads from her old friends in Trinidad, memes from which she's always trying to shove in my face. One day she tells me, "We have to shut the windows tonight because there will be helicopters spraying the whole city for Covid-19."

"That's crazy," I tell her, realizing that if I weren't there she'd think it was true.

I had had a flight back to Copenhagen for mid-May, but in light of the pandemic, the flight kept on getting canceled until it was pushed back to September, which was finally canceled as well.

I had never fully realized how much my mother's anxieties had affected me. It wasn't until I spent this lockdown time with her that I realized how much her fear had impeded me. Living in an abusive household had left its mark on all of us — but while my siblings and I had developed a way to discuss it so that we could support each other on our own individual journey's as well as each other's, my mother has refused to entertain any mention of our shared past.

"Have you thought about going to therapy?" I asked my mother, thinking about my friend Chris and he and his family's prioritizing of healing. "You know that you've been affected by the years you lived with daddy, right?"

"I know," my mother says, her voice soft. "I would love to go to therapy," she said, "but I don't know how." I understood my mother's inability to access mental health support. It is the reality of anyone who have found themselves with limited resources. I wanted more than anything to offer my mother support, to "save" her. But my own reality wasn't much different from hers. The truth was, whatever issues my family had endured, they impacted us in ways that greatly debilitated our ability to support each other. This was one of the areas that had greatly saddened my grandmother. To hear her tell it, as she often did, family was supposed to support each other. However, in my family, petty competition and rivalry — primarily in my mother's generation — greatly impeded us in working with any cohesion.

I took my boxes of letters and journals and burned them in a neighbor's backyard. I didn't need them anymore. They had done their job. Those papers were the archive of a life that I had once lived. I took a deep breath and smiled. I thought about that little girl I had found in that picture: we had made it and there was still so much to learn.

While I had been there, federal troops had descended on Portland, and there were reports that citizens of this country were being snatched by unmarked soldiers, put into unmarked cars and taken to unknown places. Trump had threatened to do the same in so-called "anarchist states" such as New York, Seattle and Portland. If there was one thing I took away from being on lockdown in New York, it's that the activist community is strong there. Mutual Aid and direct action abounds — and it's heartwarming to observe how folks come together instead of resorting to discord and disruption.

Kelly had been trying to get me out to Oakland for the longest time, and when I realized that I would not be able to head back to Copenhagen any time soon, I decided to fly out to Oakland in the middle of the pandemic. I bought a ticket with some credit I had with JetBlue and flew out to San Francisco a week later, and I've been in Oakland ever since.

Here in Oakland the air is dark from the recent spate of wildfires. The hills of Turtle Island are all around me, reminding me that I am not too far from my ancestral home.

It's easy to walk with my head held high here; the Ohlone ancestors speak to me through the red woods and eucalyptus trees that I spy among the magnolias. Dandelions grow among irises and I continue my ritual of toning my nervous system by drinking chamomile tea. Here in California, marijuana has been decriminalized and I enjoy walking into a store to get my plant medicine needs.

***

I am deeply grateful to my mother for keeping the boxes for all that time. I got an opportunity to look back into my past, and see my past — ironically enough, as this is the year that it happened — with 20/20 vision. I found all my old stories, including my first published piece, "Take Time to Listen." I was in high school when I wrote it. I had this idea about a girl and her best friend, Gary. Gary was gay, and she didn't know — the story revolved around his coming out to her. It got published in the school magazine, but I remember my tenth-grade English teacher, Mrs. Radcliffe, verbally expressing that she did not believe I had written the story and that, if I had, it had to have been something I had experienced. Both of her assumptions were wrong.

It would still be another few months until I could finally board a plane and head back to Copenhagen. But I was ready to return. I was healthier — mentally, spiritually, physically and emotionally — than I'd ever been, and I was more committed to creating a life for myself. What that is, precisely, I'm still not sure. But I do know it involves a home in the Danish countryside (for now), and a trip back to Trinidad, of course. Hopefully, someday sooner than later, I'll create that opportunity to put Masanobu Fukuoka's ideas to work.

Before I leave Oakland, Keiko shows up in the garden one day as I sat, communing with my grandmother and admiring a hummingbird suspended right above a papyrus plant. "This is for you," she says as she hands me a white furry thing. "It's a fox fur." I accept the gift and the long coat unfurled from my arms. "It's from a matriarch from the neighborhood," she tells me, "Annie Hatchett. Originally from Texas, she lived until she was ninety-nine." I tried the coat on and smiled. I guess my grandmother really did hear my mother and I that day on her deathbed.

Another departure gift I receive before I leave Oakland, is a small paper crane from Jun Hamamoto, who is a social justice advocate. She has been teaching at San Quentin Prison for over twenty years and is an art instructor there and a member of the San Quentin Buddhist sangha. She believes in the healing and transforming power of art and continues to work with and uplift her formerly incarcerated students, many of whom are at risk of deportation. Jun combines social justice with direct action to practice engaged Buddhism, is a dharma school teacher and was ordained by Zen master Thích Nhất Hạnh. Hanging from the paper crane was the note: "Home is everywhere I am."

Acknowledgments

Amber Payne & Rayner Ramirez & Ruby
Jaishri Abichandani
Jakob's Eye
Shelley-Ann Balbirsingh D'Anna
Kelly Curry
Ida Marie Therkildsen
Mary Beth Yarrow
Christopher Yarrow
Jay Braun
Richard O'Connor
Keiko Kubo
Christian Von Staffeldt
Beryl Balbirsingh
Gillian Goddard
Günay Usta
Lisa Davis

&

Marie D. Brown

Repeater Books

is dedicated to the creation of a new reality. The landscape of twenty-first-century arts and letters is faded and inert, riven by fashionable cynicism, egotistical self-reference and a nostalgia for the recent past. Repeater intends to add its voice to those movements that wish to enter history and assert control over its currents, gathering together scattered and isolated voices with those who have already called for an escape from Capitalist Realism. Our desire is to publish in every sphere and genre, combining vigorous dissent and a pragmatic willingness to succeed where messianic abstraction and quiescent co-option have stalled: abstention is not an option: we are alive and we don't agree